'Within these pages Andy creatively, and powerfully, challenges us, saying that not only does everyone love a good story but everyone lives by a story. Then he inspirationally invites us to join in with what might possibly be the greatest, truest and most important story ever told, the one with the biggest impact on our lives. Miss it! Miss out!'

Matt Summerfield

'From the opening paragraph, I was hooked. Let me just say that, if you've ever asked the big questions about life and wondered what on earth it's all about, this is a must read for you and your friends.'

Carl Beech

'Unpacks the various stories that society urges us to live by and helps us to understand the truth and impact on our lives of the God story.'

Rob Parsons, OBE

'Encouraging and accessible. This book will bring you closer to God, the ultimate storyteller.'

Pete Greig

'Fuelled by the belief that we are created for purpose, Andy Frost lays out a compelling plea for us to consider the narrative of our lives. Are we going to settle for less? Be short-changed by the immediate offers around us? This book encourages us to discover that there is a greater narrative at work that we have the opportunity to be written into – ultimately, we will find the real meaning for our existence.'

Lou Fellingham

'Such a great read! It's pacey and accessible and Andy manages to address the heavy questions of life but with a light touch. Whatever age or stage you're at, this book is invaluable in discovering, or finding again, your Story.'

Tim Hughes

Andy Frost is Director of Share Jesus International and is responsible for kick-starting a variety of projects that help the Church to communicate the story of Jesus. He is a popular speaker and the author of a number of books, and has presented *Jesus. The Series*.

He is married to Jo and they have two daughters. Currently living in London, Andy loves travelling the world, surfing good waves, pushing himself in physical challenges and eating Mexican food.

Follow him on Twitter @andythefrosty.

LONG STORY SHORT
FINDING YOUR PLACE IN GOD'S UNFOLDING STORY

ANDY FROST

First published in Great Britain in 2018

Society for Promoting Christian Knowledge
36 Causton Street
London SW1P 4ST
www.spck.org.uk

British Library Cataloguing-in-Publication Data
A catalogue record for this book is available from the British Library

ISBN 978–0–281–07931–5
eBook ISBN 978–0–281–07932–2

1 3 5 7 9 10 8 6 4 2

Typeset by Fakenham Prepress Solutions, Fakenham, Norfolk NR21 8NN
Printed in Great Britain by Jellyfish

eBook by Fakenham Prepress Solutions, Fakenham, Norfolk NR21 8NN

Produced on paper from sustainable forests

Dedicated to my daughters, Eloise and Talitha,
that they would live wonderful, rich, profound stories
that point to the Author of all things . . .

Contents

Acknowledgements

It's been a real privilege to write this book. My hope is that it will inspire us all to live a better story.

A big thanks to all those who have helped to make this book a reality. To the team at Share Jesus International – Matt Brinkley, Jasmin Jones, Daniel Watson, Malcolm and Jeanne Claridge, and all the Trustees – thanks for believing in me and giving me the space to develop the story concepts.

A massive thanks to the team at SPCK and, in particular, to my editor Elizabeth Neep, for her wisdom, creativity and encouragement. Thanks for taking this book on!

And a big thanks to my family – the inspiration from my children, the encouragement from my wife Jo and the healthy sibling banter from my brother Chris. Cath Lyden and Jacqui Parkinson, thanks for reading some of the early drafts! Your feedback was immensely helpful.

And finally, a big thanks to God for helping me to discover my unique story . . . here's to the next chapters.

WHAT STORY IS YOUR LIFE TELLING?

Introduction

My granddad was a slender, quite serious-looking clergyman. Born in 1920, he had a Victorian air about him in his dark suits and wrinkly skin. One of his quirks was that he was a member of the Magic Circle.

He would take great delight on a Saturday afternoon in trying to teach me, a young and uncoordinated boy, magic tricks that I could then perform at family get-togethers. His magic apparatus, with its fanciful handkerchiefs and conjuring guidebooks, looked as if it had been passed on for generations. They all carried a pungent smell like historical artifacts.

It was the disappearing coin that particularly got my attention as a wide-eyed eight-year-old. I remember the first time he performed the magic trick for me and I was convinced that magic must be real. He neatly tucked an old farthing inside a patterned handkerchief, held it over a glass of water and dropped the coin in. The coin seemed to clang noisily against the side of the glass but on closer inspection, the glass was empty. The coin had vanished.

It was actually quite disheartening when he revealed that he had simply manipulated my attention, switching the coin for a replica that was made of glass, which made the same clanging effect but which of course appeared invisible in the water.

It was this art of selective attention that gripped me. It was so simple and yet could be used to profound effect. It's the way a good magician will manage your attention by getting you to focus on what they want you to focus on. And while you're focusing on that, they'll 'make the magic happen'. Abracadabra!

We live with a barrage of sensory information every day. We are forced to focus our attention on what we think is important and let other things go completely unnoticed. And with so much grabbing our attention – the bank balance that is never as big as we'd like, the daily nagging of an inbox that is never quite empty, the to-do list that is never complete – we fail to notice that with each 24 hours another day disappears. And with every day that disappears, we miss the opportunity to take control of the direction of our life stories.

You see, every life tells a story. The twists and the turns, the hurts and the pains, the moments of triumph and the moments of tragedy are like a series of film frames that collectively encapsulate the story of your life. Some of our life stories are straightforward, others are more convoluted and some are more like a collection of short stories stitched together like a sweater that your auntie lovingly knitted for you one Christmas.

And here's the thing. What if the mind-bending illusions and the 'magic' words, the bank balance and the email inbox distract us from living a good story?

This book is about the one big question that I believe we need to ask: 'What story is my life telling?'

WE ARE ALL BORN INTO A MUCH BIGGER STORY. WHAT STORIES FRAME OUR LIFE STORIES?

Chapter one

ONCE UPON A TIME . . .

Man is always a teller of tales. He lives surrounded by his stories . . .
he sees everything that happens to him through them and he tries
to live his own life as if he were telling a story.

Jean-Paul Sartre

The way I see it, life is short. At the time of writing, the average
life expectancy in the UK is a meagre 81.5 years. Broken down,
that's 978 months, 4,250 weeks or 29,747 days. Given the brevity
of life and the enormity of all the world has to offer, each of us
will only ever experience a tiny fraction of all that can be experienced. And the cruel part is, we never know just how long we
have left. Death could come a-knocking at any moment. None of
us knows when our end credits will roll.

We measure age in the number of years that we have lived, but
I wonder what the impact on our thinking would be if we were
able to measure it in the number of days, weeks, months and years
that we have left. How might that change the story we are telling?
Would it move things up a gear, having that fresh perspective?

There can be something beautiful about funerals. Now, don't get me wrong, funerals are often the hardest of events, brimming with grief, loss and a sense of questioning. But funerals can also meddle with our perspective for the better. Funerals can be a healthy reminder that death is on its way. Just like a JCB digger forcing away the topsoil of pleasantries and superficiality, they can brutally and beautifully create space for each of us to look into our souls.

As the eulogy is given, we are made to remember our own mortality. Often with a mix of tears and laughter, we reminisce over someone's life story, we celebrate the good they did and the adventures they lived. And sometimes we are left wondering, how will we be remembered? We wonder what story will be told about our lives.

There is now an app for your phone that, taking into account your vital statistics, gives you a predicted countdown on how many days, hours and minutes you have left before you die. This may sound scary, but the intention behind it is to encourage you to embrace a healthier lifestyle and thereby extend your life. The app might help us focus on living well – but it really is just a 'guess-timate'; without a definite countdown it is impossible to know when our time may be up.

Ultimately, the future is a mystery. We live in the uncertainty of not knowing just how long we have left. What we do have is the power to choose, in the here and now of today, how our life story will play out. Today, as another of our possible 29,747 days gets invested in the slot machine of life, we may not be able to choose exactly what we live, but we can choose *how* we live.

★

There is a famous scene in the 1970s zombie film *Dawn of the Dead* where two of the lead characters, Francine and Stephen, look down from the rooftop of a shopping mall to see zombies roaming around trying to get into the shops. With a sense of disbelief, Francine asks, 'What are they doing? Why do they come here?' Stephen responds, 'Some kind of instinct. Memory of what they used to do. This was an important place in their lives.' It became a classic scene in movie history because it prophetically depicts the living dead – people who have many of the attributes of being alive but no sense of meaning or purpose. People existing rather than living.

Though we wouldn't like to admit it, this sentiment can be seen in many aspects of our own lives. We may post on social media so that people can 'like' us without even thinking of whether it really matters. Or we might operate on autopilot, switching on the TV as soon as we arrive home because we'd rather busy our minds with stories of others than fully engage with our own. We look to the sleight of hand again and again, even when we know deep down that the true magic isn't to be found there.

I wonder, sometimes, if the sleight of hand has left us focusing on the wrong things and missing out on what life is all about. But how do we avoid focusing on the wrong things? How do we make sure that we don't live life on autopilot? Ultimately, how do we find a story worth living?

JOURNEY

This book is a journey into the world of stories. We're going to begin by looking at why stories are so important, then we're going to explore the three main stories we tell ourselves over and over again in the Western world.

First, there is the story of happiness: that life is about enjoying what is on offer. Like squeezing the last bit of toothpaste out of a tube, life is for squeezing every bit of pleasure out of our short time here on earth. The second is about safety. The world is a scary, messed-up place and the aim of the game is to try to make ourselves as safe as we can. The third story that I believe we live for in the West is the narrative about significance. We want our life story to have mattered. And if our existence is just some great accident, then we have to create meaning and purpose so that we can find some kind of significance in the story we live.

The next three chapters are an exploration of these commonly held stories. They present an opportunity to think about the story your life is telling and what you really want it to say. We'll then move on to the whole idea of meta-narratives – the idea that there are bigger stories that frame the smaller stories we tell ourselves every day.

And then I will pitch you the God story – the story we find in the pages of the Bible. This is the story I have chosen to frame my own life and I will offer you my reasoning as to why I think it makes sense. From this point, I want to explore what the God story means for our lives. I will explore God as the central character. I will explain why I don't think we are meant to be the centre of our story, and how there is something beautiful about discovering what it means for us to be a character in *his* story. We'll then get really practical in the last couple of chapters, looking at our unique role in history, and how we can discover our subplot in God's unfolding narrative.

THE POWER OF STORY

Before digging deeper into the God story, or even our personal stories, it helps to see just how important stories are. Whether or not you are 'a reader' doesn't matter, because it's impossible to deny that stories are everywhere. We often think of stories being entombed in books and films, but the truth is, stories are all around us.

Every day we receive dozens of stories from the adverts that adorn street hoardings, our TV screens and our social media channels. It's fascinating how advertisers frequently don't even feature the product in the commercial; instead they tell us a story rich in emotion that somehow connects with our very being. As McDonald's celebrated its fortieth anniversary, there were no perfect photographs of a Big Mac positioned next to a cold Coke, condensation running down the side of the cup. Instead, there were a series of images that depicted milestone moments.

The 'brave little soldier treat' photograph showed a young boy in the back of the car with his arm in plaster, a Happy Meal just in view. The 'just passed your driving test drive-thru' depicted a young driver with a perfectly positioned green 'P' plate driving past a McDonald's serving window. The campaign was not directly selling us burgers but telling us stories that would engage with our emotions, reminding us of deep memories. They were helping us associate the golden arches brand with key life moments, in turn writing McDonald's into our own memories.

Our news media pump us with stories whenever we glance at a screen or wade through a paper. Whichever incident is being reported, the coverage we choose to follow dictates the story that is being told. The reporters tell us who are the good guys and who are the bad guys. These stories saturate our lives.

Most days we pass by without thinking about the monuments and graveyards that punctuate our cities, towns and villages. Interestingly, commemorative monuments are nearly always built by the victors, reinforcing a story that might not be wholly true. These monuments remind us of our past, the cost of freedom, the heroes of history. And graveyards remind us of our future, our mortality, our 81.5 years. Our life story might one day just become a short epitaph on a moss-covered gravestone hiding in the shadows of an overgrown cemetery.

The songs we sing, the box sets we watch, the clothes we wear, the shopping centres we frequent, the people we live with, the coffee we drink – all these tell a story. Stories are the glue that shape our conversations, our interactions and our very thoughts. The poet Muriel Rukeyser famously unpacked the idea that the universe is not really made of atoms but of stories. For Rukeyser, they are the heartbeat of our very existence, but what makes stories so powerful?

STORIES GIVE CONTEXT

First, stories give context. They help us make order out of chaos. Whenever we see something unusual or unexpected, like a broken-down car, we say, 'I wonder what's happened there?' We yearn for a story to help us make sense of what we have witnessed. Stories help us understand what's going on.

I was gripped when I first started reading Dean Karnazes' book *Ultramarathon Man*. He begins with the description of a random conversation he has with a pizza delivery man. It's nearing midnight and Dean is ordering pizza for himself; but he doesn't order a pizza for one but a family-sized pizza. Then he goes on to order not just one piece of cheesecake but an entire cheesecake. And on top of that he asks for a flask of coffee.

The already confused pizzeria man now asks for the delivery address, and Dean says that he wants it to be delivered to the edge of a highway, miles from the nearest houses. The scene, as it unfolds, leaves the reader confused too, until you discover that Dean is an ultra-marathon runner, running 170 miles straight through the night. He is desperate for calories to keep himself going. As the pizza is delivered, he rolls it up in one hand like a taco and carries on running off into the night, munching away. The story gives context. It helps us understand what's going on.

Somewhere between Babygros and mastering the alphabet in nursery, children embark on a stage of life where they want to question *everything*. My daughter was no exception. When she was two, she would often ask, 'Can you tell me a story about that?'

Even as a toddler she understood that within the context of a story, complex things could begin to make more sense.

As we search for our life story, we become aware that we find ourselves in a bigger story that gives our life context. We have all been brought up with some kind of understanding of family that has shaped our worldview. The values of our parents, the things we experienced, the religious systems we grew up with, the very fact that our families were present or distant, all frame our life's story. Whenever life stories are retold in books, documentaries or films, they often pinpoint a key moment in childhood – when a wrong was witnessed, a passion was birthed or a skill noticed – that changed the trajectory of the individual's life, either for good or for evil.

But more than just family, the community that surrounds us in our formative years, with both its generosity and its prejudice, will give us a backdrop to understanding our life story. And more than family and local community, we are born into a much bigger story – one that is being played out among nations and multi-nationals framed by human history. Now as never before we live in a time period when technology is king and the world's issues are available online for all to see in HD quality.

Part of discerning our story is discerning the bigger story in which we find ourselves. It's about understanding our context and the story that has been spoken over our lives.

STORIES GET BENEATH OUR SKIN

But stories do more than give us context. They have the ability to move us to tears and to laughter. Stories get beneath our skin.

In the world of child psychology, the power of story is being realized. Children with behavioural problems, for example, often find it hard to express themselves with words. When talking through issues they can feel pressurized, almost as if they are being interrogated, and so there is a growing trend towards 'play therapy'. Through role play and storytelling, children are given a freedom to explore emotions and express feelings. Creating stories with figurines or painting or acting out scenarios can give children the chance to operate at their own pace and process emotions they would otherwise find difficult to articulate. Stories have the power to open that vault of emotions we sometimes want to keep firmly closed.

Stories also have the potential to be emotive enough to challenge our very core; we get transported into an experience of life in somebody else's shoes. Many stories that have been told brilliantly in books and on cinema screens have changed perceptions on issues such as gender, race and culture. As readers and audiences emotionally experience the reality of other people's existence, mindsets can be transformed.

The power of story in changing belief systems was particularly well executed in a number of British university cities in 1984, a time when apartheid still existed in South Africa. Barclays was involved in maintaining the system of apartheid in its banks, where 'Whites Only' signs were customary. In the UK activists took to retelling this story using graffiti. Where there were pairs of Barclays ATM machines, above one was spray-painted the word 'blacks' and above the other 'whites only'. This one act of defiance enabled people to experience the story of apartheid bringing the evil reality of a distant land into the sharp focus on our shores. It left people feeling unsettled, and the knock-on effect was that fewer graduates applied to work at Barclays and students refused to bank with Barclays. By 1986, Barclays had pulled out of its investment in South Africa.

Finding our story is in part about understanding what makes us tick. It's about discovering our passions, our needs, our humanity. Stories allow us to be immersed, to have our emotions meddled with and our hearts changed. That is the power of story.

STORIES HELP US UNDERSTAND WHAT WE WANT

Stories give context. Stories enable us to experience. And stories help us understand what we want.

It was Joseph Campbell, author of *The Hero with a Thousand Faces*, who first articulated the idea that although all civilizations create their own stories, clothed in their own cultural nuances, in fact every story has the same basic structure. He argued that the basic structure of any good story involves the journey of a hero.

The first fundamental part is that the hero must want something – whether it's to find love, win the FA Cup or stop an alien invasion. Think of any great film and you will instantly know what the hero wants. Dory wants to find Nemo. Marty wants to get back to the future. James Bond wants to stop the bad guys. The hero wants something.

The second fundamental part is that the hero, driven by a need, has to move into an unfamiliar situation and adapt to it. The protagonist, desperate for love, sets out on a blind date; a football player eager for success leaves his family to join a new club; or our hero climbs aboard a new spaceship in want of adventure. For the story to be really moving, the new surroundings will create significant conflict and challenge, pushing the hero to the edge of their capabilities. Story consultant and university professor Bobette Buster, who has worked in the film industry with Pixar, Disney and Sony, puts it like this: 'If you want to turn a nice guy into a hero, you've got to put him through hell. It's in this furnace of challenge that the true colours of the hero are revealed.'[1]

Third, after the want and the challenge, the hero gets what they desire – though it might not be what they first set out for. For the story to be compelling, the cost must be great. The character desperate for love finds the perfect soulmate but has to deal with his own selfishness in order to win her over. The footballer faces criticism, almost gives up and has to train harder than ever; he fails to win the FA Cup but discovers that success is about more than trophies – it is about being the best he can be. The hero loses her comrades to obscure penguin lookalike aliens but manages to protect planet Earth.

Finally, the fourth part of the story is about the hero returning to familiarity, having been changed by the experience. The groom gives his speech on the wedding day. The footballer is back with his family. The spaceship lands to cheering crowds.

This basic structure has been utilized by numerous great storytellers over the last 60 years. George Lucas, creator of the Star Wars films, refers to Joseph Campbell as 'my Yoda', highlighting the significant role the author played in explaining the science behind good stories.

You see, stories help us understand what we want – how we can be a hero. They help us navigate the choices we have to make every day. This simple premise, that a good story is about a character who wants something and has to overcome conflict to get it, helps us live a good story.

The problem comes when we don't want something significant. The story of a character who just wants a nice holiday isn't particularly compelling – a holiday doesn't seem that important. At the same time, wanting something significant is not enough. If the main character doesn't have to overcome some kind of difficulty to get what she wants, then the odds are it's a pretty boring story. The story of a millionaire doing good to others will not be interesting if it costs her nothing more than some spare pocket change. There is no conflict. Compelling stories combine a noble cause alongside real conflict.

BUT I DON'T KNOW WHAT I WANT

In reality, we aren't always conscious of what we want; we may not know what the narrative is that is driving our story. Sometimes we avoid asking the uncomfortable questions and skip over the conflicts in our lives.

There is a famous saying, that the two most important days in your life are the day you are born, and the day you find out why. There's some real truth in that. We often float through life until the day we discover a cause worth living and dying for – something that makes life more consistent, rather than a series of film frames. But the issue is that very few people have a day when everything suddenly becomes clear. A lot more common, I think, are smaller moments of clarity when we discover a little more of our calling, our purpose, the story for our lives. These moments allow us to position ourselves for what might be in store next.

The philosopher James Bryan Smith writes:'Narrative is the central function . . . of the human mind. We turn everything into a story in order to make sense of life. We dream in narrative, day-dream in narrative, remember, anticipate, hope, despair, believe, doubt, plan, revise, criticize, construct, gossip, learn, hate and love by narrative. In fact, we cannot avoid it. We are storied creatures.'[2] As storied creatures, perhaps we need to turn off the autopilot, being proactive rather than merely playing the role that society presumes of us. Maybe it's time to be more aware of selective attention – to make sure we aren't duped into becoming the living dead transfixed by our smartphones.

Stories help us understand why someone would want a pizza delivered to the edge of a motorway at midnight. Stories move us and change mindsets. And stories help us understand what we want, whether that is to fight off aliens or battle real-life issues like extreme poverty. Now let's take this gift of life seriously and live the greatest story possible.

The story we choose for our lives has huge ramifications. Our story will direct how we live out our time on earth and ultimately will determine how we view ourselves. And with this as our backdrop, and the three stories that I think we live for in the Western world as our starting point, let's explore how we begin to find a story for our lives.

THE HAPPINESS
STORY IS ALMOST
HYPNOTIC IN THE
WAY IT ENTICES US. IT
CAN EASILY BECOME
OUR RIGHT, OUR
DESTINATION, OUR
FANTASY, OUR STORY.

Chapter two

BE HAPPY

Don't worry, be happy.

Bobby McFerrin

He had it all. Looks. Style. Charisma. Oh, and he was heir to a 50 million dollar fortune. Bunker Spreckels has gone down in history as one of the world's greatest hedonists. He lived fast and died young. The 2016 film *Bunker 77* celebrated the life of the 'young American rebel seeking freedom, love, and authenticity in a chaotic world'.

Born in 1949, he grew up living in luxury, with film idol Clark Gable as his stepfather. He dated Miss Teen California, became a nationally ranked archer and was all set to become a stockbroker. Then he turned his back on the success he was destined for and became an itinerant surfer living on the coast of Hawaii. At 21 he received his vast inheritance from his father's sugar business and became a controversial surf star. Known for his originality and charisma he took to a world of excess. He travelled, immersing himself in the drug scene and partying hard. He died aged 27 but his short life story has become legendary.

The happiness story is almost hypnotic in the way it entices us. Be happy. Do whatever makes you happy. Our culture celebrates those who follow this track. And I get it. There is a part of me that loves this narrative. The world offers so much to explore, to taste, to experience. And there is something attractive about those who choose to abandon conventional lifestyles and travel the world sampling the delights that are out there, getting drunk on adventure and perfect sunsets.

'And they lived happily ever after' – or so the fairytale ends. We have been drip-fed these happiness stories from birth. Stories that end neatly when the witch has been dealt with and the prince and princess walk arm in arm down the aisle together. Happiness is the story we often search for to frame our lives in the Western world. A vision of the good life – the subject of countless books peddled by self-help gurus and perfect lifestyles promoted by advertising executives. Happiness can easily be seen as our right, our destination, our fantasy, our story.

Many of us live by this story. Life is about pursuing happiness. And it's no surprise. We live in a world that ruthlessly tries to eliminate discomfort, where technology does our mundane tasks and where air conditioning, fridge freezers and Siri make life much easier than it was in previous centuries. We immerse ourselves in Hollywood movies and TV shows that meddle with our emotions and send us yearning for wealth and success. We spend our time being mesmerized by social media, looking at a distorted reality of old acquaintances who, with just the right filter, leave us thinking we're missing out.

The happiness story gets under our skin. Our lives are lived with the mantra, 'If it makes me happy and it doesn't make other people unhappy, I'll do it.' And as we pursue happiness, we look to the immediate, living for the moment. It's all about the now. On a Saturday night in bars and clubs across the globe, this pursuit of happiness is lived out. Lines of shot glasses, drunken one-night stands without thinking through the physical and emotional wreck of tomorrow. Overconsumption gone mad.

This kind of short-term thinking and self-centred pleasure-seeking is often called hedonism. But it's not just about Jaeger Bombs and Beer Pong. The 'live for the moment' motif is lived out in the thrill of a shopping spree without a thought about next month's credit card bill or the buzz of late-night online gambling with buy-ins you can't afford. Happiness is about squeezing all life has to offer in the moment. The future is uncertain. Tomorrow we die, so let's eat, drink and be merry.

IN SEARCH OF HAPPINESS – NOW OR LATER?

For some, happiness is about abandoning the future to live in the moment. But many more of us adopt the story of happiness that does the exact opposite. We actually abandon the present and live for the future. Happiness lies just around the next corner – in the future and just out of reach.

We live under the expectations of others. If only we can achieve enough and be successful in their eyes, then we will be happy. Looking to the future for happiness means that our story is about what needs to be done now to one day enjoy the rewards of our labour. We define happiness in terms of prosperity and success, a paid-off mortgage and accolades from others.

★

The mist clung to the mountains as we approached our final ascent. Scafell Pike was the second and trickiest of three climbs in under 24 hours. The Three Peaks Challenge is as tough as it is well known. Walking through the night, landscapes can be deceptive. We soon realized that the peak we had seen was not the final peak but another undulation. As soon as we had reached it, a higher peak emerged from the mist. And as we reached the next 'summit', mockingly another peak revealed itself from behind the curtains of the night sky.

This is what it's like for those who are always looking to the future for happiness. It's just around the corner. I hear it all the time. I will be so happy and can enjoy life when I've finished my exams. Or when I have earned some money. Or when I have secured my promotion. Or when I have bought a property. Or when I have a family. Or when my children are in school. Or maybe, one day, when I retire. We seem to have swallowed a lie that tells us to delay all gratification. Rather than enjoying what we have, we push for the next promotion, the faster car and the bigger home. Because then we'll be happy.

Studies show that people are happier when they have shorter commutes, but as they climb the career ladder they opt for bigger homes in suburbia which means longer journeys. People tend to stay in jobs they hate that cause stress they can't stand because the pay packet is good – and downsizing would surely mean we'd failed.

Those of us who live for the future think that one day we'll be happy, when success is finally achieved. That title, that bank balance, that lifestyle. The scary thing is that those who finally reach what they think is the pinnacle of success, that moment of happiness, often feel bitterly disappointed.

Perhaps nowhere is this more evident that in the world of sports. Olympians train for years for the right to compete. The competition itself can last a mere handful of seconds, as they dive into the pool or race the 110-metre hurdles. And in the minutest of actions or a fraction of a second, they may miss out on that sought-after medal around their neck, devastated.

But even those who win gold, as they stand on the podium listening to their national anthem, realize that this is it. This is what they have been working for all those years. And it's over in a moment. Physically and psychologically drained, this season of life comes to an end as their national flag is raised overhead. People call it post-Olympic depression.

The US swimmer Allison Schmitt won five medals, three of them gold, at London 2012, and set a new world record. She was undeniably successful, but following the games she suffered serious depression. In a television interview, she said: 'I didn't want to show my weakness. I didn't want to ask for help, but in this situation I found out . . . that I couldn't keep fighting it by myself. There's this thing that they call post-Olympic blues and I think I had a little bit of that and I kept isolating myself.'[3]

Success alone is not all it's made out to be. And perhaps for those that get there it's harder than for those who invest their lives striving for it but will never realize how unfulfilling it is. The self-styled philosopher Russell Brand writes in his book *Revolution*: 'If taking drugs worked I'd still be doing it, if promiscuous sex was continually fulfilling I'd've carried on, if fame and fortune were the answer I'd hurl this laptop out of the window and get on with making movies. They don't work.'[4]

One of my favourite fables is of an American investment banker who finds himself on a beautiful beach in Mexico. A small boat arrives on the beach with just one fisherman aboard. Inside the boat are several large fish. The investment banker compliments the fisherman on his catch but asks why he is not still out there catching more fish. The fisherman explains that he has caught enough fish to support his family. He doesn't need to work any longer. Instead he can enjoy his day, hang out with his kids and spend time with his wife.

The American doesn't understand. He suggests the fisherman fish some more and make some money. Then the fisherman could buy a bigger boat and employ others. In time he could own several boats, and with a greater catch, sell direct to the wholesaler. He could end up being very rich. The fisherman looks bemused and replies, 'But then what?' 'Well, then you could retire, enjoy your days, hang out with your kids and spend time with your wife.' The fisherman's retort? 'But that's exactly what I'm doing now.'

The hedonistic approach of living in the now and the idea of waiting to enjoy life in the future are like the two extremes of a pendulum we try to ride. We want to balance living in the moment with working for what lies ahead. Happiness is our story.

REALITY CHECK

But here's the thing: what does happiness look like? Can it be measured? Will we ever achieve a perfect state of happiness?

Many of us have never really explored happiness. We have not thought through what it means to be happy. It can be defined as an emotion – a feeling of pleasure or contentment. Does this mean that we one day arrive at a euphoric state, moving from bliss to greater levels of bliss?

Unfortunately not. The truth is, there will always be pain and heartache in life. The word 'happy' comes from the old English 'hap' meaning luck. It's where we get our words hapless and haphazard. Perhaps when we try to describe living a happy life we are actually talking about playing the odds, riding our luck, making sure we get more than our fair share of laughter, success and positive vibes.

And when it comes to measuring happiness, it's very subjective. Ascertaining our level of happiness requires us to reflect on our lives. Research shows that we are disproportionately affected by the most recent events in our lives, so if we are going through a happy spell, we are more likely to feel that we are a happy person.

The problem with happiness as a narrative for our lives is that it is a mirage. We can never be fully happy. Scientists believe that our level of happiness is actually preset. Our biology determines our emotional state, and circumstances and our reaction to them have only a fractional impact. You may think that winning the lottery would make you much happier, while losing the ability to use your legs would make you a lot less happy, but experiments suggest that you gradually adapt to new circumstances and your happiness levels remain about the same.

A great analogy is the beauty of a warm fire on a cold day. You have been out walking in the bitter wind and fresh snow. You enter a traditional English pub and find a roaring fire. With your favourite drink, you position yourself next to the flickering flames to enjoy the heat on offer. And as you sink into the worn chair, you think to yourself, this is the best fire ever. But within ten minutes, you have adjusted to the warmth. You find the fire too hot. And you reposition yourself in a different part of the pub. You have adjusted to the new circumstances.

Whether we are chasing the immediate, playing the long game or trying to enjoy the now with an eye on the future, happiness alone is not a big enough story. Too many of us, perhaps subconsciously, make happiness the pursuit of our lives – but happiness is not enough.

THE DARK SIDE OF HAPPINESS

It was Sigmund Freud who taught that what humans wanted most in life was pleasure. But one day an old student of his, psychologist Viktor Frankl, stood up to Freud, arguing that what people ultimately want is purpose. It's when they can't find a deep sense of meaning that they distract themselves with pleasure. Frankl argued that the happiness story doesn't deliver.

Not only does the happiness story fail to deliver, it can also become dangerous. We may end up comparing our state of contentment with that of our friends and family, or start measuring our emotional state with how happy others appear. You have had a great holiday but the pictures of your friend's trip to the Maldives make you green with envy. You're loving work but the news of friends getting married and having babies makes you feel that you're going to be left on the shelf. You're chuffed at finishing your first 5K but then you see your colleagues are posting about their half marathons. And when our lives don't match up to others' photoshopped reality, we can end up depressed, feeling as if we have failed. Comparison instantly kills the joy in what we have.

And if happiness is the end goal, then our moral compass can easily get hijacked. Websites have been designed to cater for those seeking to have an affair. We wear clothes that make us feel good, with the right price tag, but they have been created in sweatshops in Asia. We use others, pushing them to one side, to get what we want. If happiness is the priority, then we no longer need to do what is right. It can lead to putting self first in such a way that it damages relationships, families and communities.

In parenting circles, parents often say that they just want their children to be happy. But is this what we really want? What if they are happy but living out their lives as selfish, abusive dictators? I'm sure we wouldn't be satisfied with this. Much more than just being happy, we want our children to be considerate people, to have a clear sense of right and wrong and to act accordingly.

You see, the happiness story is a fake. Now this doesn't mean that we all need to don sackcloth and live miserably. I believe we are to enjoy life. That feeling as the endorphins kick in after a good long run as the sunlight flickers through the trees. That sense of contentment on a spring evening with the barbecue alight and the smell of freshly cooked food filling the taste buds with expectancy. The enjoyment that a beautiful dress or a smart suit gives you when you wear it out for the first time. That sense of pleasure, a job well done, as you finish a piece of work, close the laptop and leave the office for the night.

We should enjoy what we have, but happiness can't be our *raison d'être*. If the end goal is happiness alone, our lives are focused on ourselves. We end up partying with no real purpose, searching for a reality that always eludes us. We live for the next moment of success, which just leaves us hungry for more. We find ourselves at the very centre of our story with an insatiable appetite for something that can never fully be realized. Our identity becomes dictated by our emotions.

Happiness is too small a story. But maybe, in the chapters ahead, we will discover that we were made for a bigger story. A story where happiness is not the objective, and where joy is a by-product of a very different agenda.

MANY OF US STRIVE FOR SAFETY, LIVING OUR LIVES IN FEAR. BUT THE WORLD IS CHANGING AND WE CAN'T STOP IT.

Chapter three

SAFETY FIRST

The desire for safety stands against every great and noble enterprise.

Tacitus

We were a couple of miles from land. Chomp had been deposited over the side of the boat: a mixture of fish heads and guts, which left a smelly oily residue on the surface of the ocean. Within a few moments, two Great Whites were circling the boat, on the hunt for food. It was time for the first volunteers to climb into the cage.

Over the 20 years that I have been an avid surfer I have had a couple of close encounters with finned predators. And in this moment I was coming face to face with one of my greatest fears. As the cage was brought out, I suddenly had second thoughts. I'd always wanted to go cage-diving as Great Whites swam around me. Of course I'd watched the YouTube clips where everything goes horribly wrong, but this once-in-a-lifetime opportunity I was not going to miss.

Finding the cheapest shark-diving operator had seemed a good idea, but as the cage was revealed I wondered if this was the best money-saving scheme. The cage looked like two shopping trolleys welded together as it was gently lowered into the pristine water alongside the boat. Submerged and breathing through a snorkelling mask, I was mesmerized as the sharks swam majestically past showcasing their raw power, gliding through the water at menacing speed. It was like being in a zoo, but the other way round. It didn't feel particularly safe but in that moment I felt fully alive, blood pulsating around my veins.

The world is not safe. Whenever I am surfing in the murky water in warmer climates, I am constantly aware of what could be lurking beneath the surface. But there is a choice to make. The thrill of sliding down walls of water always carries with it a certain risk. The truth is, we encounter risks every day. The chance of being killed crossing the road or slipping in the bath are far greater than becoming fish food. But fear is powerful.

Scientists have found that we are born with only two fears: the fear of falling and the fear of loud noises. As we grow up we adopt a multitude of fears. We learn to fear things, and these fears come from the story we inhabit. In our family unit, we pick up on cues from our parents that teach us what we need to fear. It could be fear of spiders or fear of the dark. And in our culture at large we learn from the evidence of our environment about wider societal fears. It could be the fear of terrorist attack or fear of another recession.

Now fear has its uses. Fear is our friend in that it acts as a survival mechanism that keeps us safe. When you see or are aware of something to be scared of, the sensory systems in your brain's amygdala kick in. They create the adrenaline response that tells your heart to beat faster and your body to sweat. At the same time, a reaction takes place in the brain's cortical centre that reasons out the risk. In that moment we choose fight or flight.

Some people love the sensation of being scared. They push themselves to the limits with an insatiable desire for highly sensational experiences. It's that rush of adrenaline that entices BASE jumpers to throw themselves off buildings and big waves surfers to chase swells around the globe in search of 80-foot waves. The more these thrill-seekers embark on death-defying stunts and survive, the more able their brains become to reason out the risk.

But most of us don't push ourselves to the edge of our fears. Each day news headlines remind us that the world is not safe. There is an ongoing threat of terrorism. There is corruption in the financial sector. Cyber attacks are ever more likely. There is no job certainty. Cancer is on the rise. The future is uncertain and we need to make ourselves as safe as we can.

Fear has its uses but it can also render us immobile because it remains one of the strongest of storylines. Fear plays out powerfully on the international stage. If a population is scared, those in power know that they can manipulate freedoms and civil liberties. Fear of the other can result in wars waged and people groups persecuted. From large-scale international power games to the slight nervousness of paddling out for a surf, fear can change the way we behave.

THINGS ARE CHANGING

We jumped into an Uber and began meandering down the narrow streets of York. The driver quickly began to tell us about the harassment he experienced from traditional cabbies around the city. That day he had received verbal abuse and the 'middle finger' as he navigated rush-hour traffic. Traditional taxi drivers did not like the new competition.

The world is changing. Uber is just another in the sequence of technological changes that are shaping the way in which we do life. When cash machines were introduced, there was uproar. What would happen to the banking experience? When cars were first taking to the roads, there was real concern. What would happen to the traditional horse and cart? And now we live in a world where people no longer buy CDs, where they do their grocery shopping online and where they watch their cab drive to their location via an app on their phone.

Not only is the world changing, it is changing fast. Bedouin tribes in North Africa have always lived nomadically. They traverse the desert landscape, looking for water and setting up camp where it can be found. But things are changing even for the Bedouin. While water remains a priority, nomadic tribes are choosing camping sites partly selected according to whether there is good internet reception for their phones.

For the first time in history, information now gets passed up the generations rather than just downwards. It used to be that the elders in a community would share with the next generation lessons about how life worked – about farming the land and navigating the seasons. But it's now the young that teach their elders on certain matters – how to do online banking, how to operate a smartphone, often sharing breaking news received through social media minutes before the traditional press follows suit.

The truth is, though, many of us don't like change. In fact we often try to disrupt it and stop it happening. Change enhances our fears and so the 'stay safe' mentality becomes a focus for our lives. We mitigate our concerns with the right insurance, the right health and safety policy and the right pension scheme.

But we can't stop change happening. Things are not safe, or foolproof. Nothing is certain. No matter what we do, the future is unpredictable. Despite this, we want to live a story for our lives that's focused upon making ourselves as financially secure as possible. We hoard and invest so that we can have stability in the future. It seems logical but the irony is that the more we have, the more we have to protect. We want to cling on to what we have accumulated and we become fearful of losing it. We may end up needing extra security for our homes, with taller fences and CCTV.

And even if we get to the point of feeling financially stable, there is always something else to fear. People know that if they can make you feel afraid, they will be able to charge you for a service. In South Africa there is a lucrative business in blood banks. Middle-class individuals, driven by the fear of not having clean blood if they ever needed a transfusion, pay to have their own blood taken and stored in case of an emergency.

Fear is no way to live. Fear robs us of the joy of today and creates in us a scarcity mentality. Like my granddad's magic, so often our fears are an illusion. We allow our minds to focus on the worst possible outcome and fail to face our fears. We let fear become the undercurrent of our lives. We become experts at reading the risk into every opportunity. And so we choose to play it safe. Rather than living full lives, we look to minimize uncertainty. And we can end up choosing a bubble-wrapped existence. The question is, how can we make sure we don't end up marching to the beat of the latest worrying news headlines?

Many cultures around the world have traditions of clear rites of passage as children move into adulthood. These involve separation from the community, a time of transition and then reintegration back into community life. In the Yao tribe in East Africa, groups of boys aged 11 are taken into the bush as part of the 'Jando experience', where they are circumcised. Over a month, as they work through the healing process, they are taught how to cook, to grow food, to look after children and be a good husband. As part of this process, they are taught how to behave within community and how to relate to their elders and contribute to meetings. When the boys are reintegrated into their community, they are subject to significantly different expectations; they are no longer children but young men.

In the West there are no such experiences that help prepare us for adulthood. I'm definitely not suggesting we should introduce circumcision for all 11-year-old boys, but there is something profound about the whole experience because through it some truths about finding a story for our lives are communicated.

Author and teacher Richard Rohr has done lots of research into initiation rites and has observed some consistent lessons that are communicated across different cultures. One is the fact that you are not in control; another is that you are going to die. They may seem rather gloomy but something powerful can be unlocked when we face up to the reality check they offer.

The fear narrative falsely says that we can be in control. It tells us that if we hoard enough we can become immune to the changes in the world. Our identity can be preserved by saving and protecting what we have and staying safe; but the truth is we are not in control. None of us knows just how long we have here on planet Earth.

THE PRISON OF FEAR

We often hide away from the reality of death. My grandparents recount stories of the corpse of a loved one being in the house for a couple of days between death and burial. It gave them time to come to terms with death. In our sanitized society, the fear narrative encourages us not to think about the ultimate reality that none of us can escape. When we base our life story on fear, we are not ultimately free. We are instead imprisoned in a story that sees the world as menacing and scary.

One of my friends once had a vision to set up a retreat centre. He had a comfortable life, a comfortable job and a comfortable existence. He had shared his vision many times with a mentor. As he sipped his tea at a meeting with her, he once again spoke of his passion, detailing the intricacies of what he wanted to see happen. His mentor's response was silence, seemingly uninterested. Over a fresh pot, he tried again to convey his excitement. And then, when he asked her why she was not also excited about the possibility, she responded with the words, 'It's boring.'

'Boring?' he retorted. 'Yes, boring,' she replied. She went on to say that his life had become so comfortable and safe that this vision he had talked about for years was never going to happen because he had no plans to do anything about it. His vision had remained a dream trapped inside his head. He had become safe. That week, my friend put his house on the market and put a deposit on a derelict farm. He stopped living the story that said, 'I want to be safe,' and went on to see his vision become reality. He chose not to live a bubble-wrapped existence.

But many of us don't seize the day, grab the bull by the horns or face our fears. We instead choose to make ourselves as safe as possible. Perhaps we stay in a job we detest and never pursue our dreams because of the possibility of failure, or we hoard cash for a tomorrow that might never come.

When people in care homes are asked to reflect upon their lives and share the wisdom they have gathered, interestingly they often talk about two things. One is that they encourage the younger generation to worry less. We spend too much time worrying about things that either never happen or we can't change anyway. Their second piece of advice is to take more risks. Their regrets are often about playing it safe, and not doing the things they always dreamt of.

The fear narrative may be strong but it is a deception – and later on we'll see how a narrative of faith can highlight fear for the lie that it is.

WE WANT OUR
LIFE STORY TO
MATTER. WE WANT
TO SOMEHOW BE
IMPORTANT. SOME
OF US SPEND OUR
LIVES CHASING
SIGNIFICANCE.

Chapter four

BECOMING SOMEBODY

For me life is continuously being hungry. The meaning of life is not simply to exist, to survive, but to move ahead, to go up, to achieve, to conquer.

Arnold Schwarzenegger

The oceanic pole of inaccessibility is the place on the earth that is furthest away from land. It is situated in the South Pacific, almost 1,700 miles from the nearest islands. It might seem like one of the most irrelevant locations on the planet but in fact its inaccessibility makes it a particularly relevant place for satellite operators.

There are presently more than 2,000 satellites travelling in orbit around the earth. Each of these satellites has a limited lifespan. Many of them work for only five years. Rather than littering space with junk when they become redundant, the satellites are brought back to earth through the atmosphere. The smaller ones burn up on entry but the bigger satellites will survive and reach the earth's surface. They are brought down to this point of inaccessibility in the South Pacific, often in a final flurry of flames, to make sure they avoid hitting populated areas. And so the ocean floor in this remote part of the planet is a burial ground for satellites.

Each satellite has a specific job. Some help us understand weather patterns and predict next Thursday's forecast. Some help us communicate on our mobile phones and find our destination using GPS. Some help us watch TV shows and check our bank balance. And some help governments spy on rogue nations using radar and infrared detectors that can see what's hiding beneath military camouflage.

Even the cheapest of these satellites costs around 50 million dollars and during their five years in service they are vitally important to the way we live. Each one is significant. But once their lifespan is up they come down to earth with a bump and join other 'has-been' satellites in a watery graveyard.

The third common story that we live for is the story of significance. We want more than happiness. We want more than safety. Like each satellite, sent off for a particular mission, we want our life story to have meaning. We want our life story to matter. We want somehow to be important.

This desire for significance can manifest itself in various different ways. We might want to make our mark in history, pushing the boundaries of technology, medicine or science. Or we might try to gain the recognition we crave through our music, our sporting prowess or our theatrical ability. Some of us spend our whole lives chasing significance. We dream about becoming somebody or achieving something, but each time what we yearn for escapes us. Our dreams fail to materialize fully.

Look what's happening in the online gaming industry. Millions of people spend more than 30 hours a week living in virtual worlds. Leading game designer Jane McGonigal believes that people are leaving the real world en masse for the virtual reality of online gaming because in the virtual world we can be 'super-empowered hopeful individuals'. In other words, we can be significant.

LOOKING INTO THE FUTURE

The significance story that many of us adopt is about feeling that what we do, in some way, matters. But what one person may define as significant another may view as meaningless. The fallacy of significance is that it is up to individuals to discern what is significant. If we want to invest our lives into something bigger than ourselves, then we need to define within ourselves what that looks like. And so defining significance for our own story is difficult. We may have a bit longer than five years, but like the satellites that orbit our planet our lives are short. And whereas the satellites are programmed with a specific purpose, it can be much harder to define our purpose, the reason for our existence.

Alfred Nobel was significant. Alfred had grown mightily rich through the invention of dynamite. But in 1888 he was given a strange reality check when he had the unusual opportunity to read his own obituary. His brother had died and a French newspaper had erroneously printed Alfred's obituary, which declared him a merchant of death. On reading this, he decided that this wasn't how he wanted to be remembered. He did not want to be significant in history books as the man who had made mass killings quicker and easier. And so he used his fortune to create the Nobel prizes for outstanding achievement in literature, peace, economics, medicine and the sciences. His life is now remembered for honouring those who benefit humanity.

It is very rare to have this opportunity to look into the future and see how we will be remembered but I doubt we would want to be known for bringing despair and destruction to the world. Living in a digital age makes us more aware than ever of the mess that the world is in, and many of us look to find our significance in changing things for the better. We want to leave the world having succeeded in doing our bit, having made a difference.

I have a friend who captains boats. Big, luxury boats – boats owned by billionaires. His job involves navigating them across the Atlantic from the luxury ports of the Mediterranean to the stunning beaches of the Caribbean, so that jet-setting high-net-worth individuals can fly in and enjoy their boats whatever the season.

He was once captaining a £27 million luxury yacht through the waters of the Mediterranean en route to Barbados for a Russian oligarch. As he was crossing through the three-metre chop and as the skies began to turn grey, he saw on the horizon a tiny colourful shape. Pulling out his binoculars, it was clear that it was a dinghy with about 20 refugees crammed on board, with waves battering the sides and spilling into the boat. Despite being under strict orders from the owners not to pick up refugees, my friend saw their lives in the balance. He sped round the small dinghy three times, which had the effect of flattening the water, and he called the coastguard, who volunteered to come and rescue the refugees.

This picture, of a superyacht worth millions of pounds that is probably only used for a couple of weeks a year alongside 20 desperate refugees clinging to a lifeboat, summarizes the injustices we see in the world. Some people have overwhelming wealth while others are living in such desperation that they are willing to board their family on a tiny dinghy and charter deadly crossings in the hope of a better life.

The context of war and crime and terrorism and corruption sparks some of us to live a story finding significance in fighting for justice. Our hearts break for those who are suffering. We look at the injustice in the world and we cannot stay silent. We want a better world. We believe a better world is possible. And we make this our life story.

In the 1940s and 1950s, the psychologist Abraham Maslow developed the concept that humans have a hierarchy of needs. These needs motivate us to act. He ranks needs in order of importance, and his theory suggests that as one set of needs is met, another set emerges. For example, our most basic need is for physical survival, for food and water. This need motivates our behaviour. But once these basic needs are met, then we need safety, protection from the elements, security, order, law and stability. After these are fulfilled, we need love and belonging, and then we desire achievement, independence, status and respect. He argues that as our needs are met we search for 'self-actualization' – realizing our personal potential. Finally comes self-transcendence, which is about valuing others above ourselves. True significance is always found beyond ourselves.

COUNT FOR SOMETHING

It was one of the most fascinating documentaries I had seen in a long time. Ten young men and women, graduates with their whole lives ahead of them, had gone out to the Middle East to fight against the Islamic State. With just two weeks of training with the local militia and the most basic of military set-ups, they headed to the front line.

Fighting gun battles in abandoned desert villages, they were putting their lives on the line. With the rat-a-tat-tat of machine gunfire in the distance, the commentator asked these young volunteers why they were here. They explained how they had witnessed the atrocities of the Islamic State on social media and their simple answer was this: 'I had to do something. I wanted my life to count for something.'

Whether or not we agree with their actions, this was self-transcendence. This was finding significance. With all the comforts that Western life has to offer, they had chosen to value others above themselves. They wanted to make a difference in the world. And this was worth risking everything for.

I have many friends who have dedicated their lives to noble causes. Finding a cure for cancer. Saving the planet. Fighting extreme poverty. Rescuing trafficked people. Caring for orphans. The inequality, misery and suffering of the world draws people into a story that a better world is possible and that significance can be found in doing their part. They follow in the footsteps of countless heroes of history, like Martin Luther King, Mother Teresa and Mahatma Gandhi. It's almost as if these icons from our history books, long dead and buried, have a power from beyond the grave to inspire generations of world-changers. Each of these twentieth-century heroes is significant for a specific cause, and their lives have brought about changes in the way we see our humanity.

Che Guevara is another iconic figure of recent history. Fifty years on from his death he remains a symbol of revolution. His face is the most replicated image of all time. He adorns art galleries, posters, T-shirts and key rings. He is sung about and written about; his life story has been retold in a two-part motion picture. He too had a vision for a better world.

As a young man Guevara worked as a doctor, serving lepers. He helped the marginalized and the oppressed. But as he got older his focus changed. He looked not to caring for the sick but to fighting against the systemic issues, as he saw them, that keep the impoverished poor. To his aunt in 1954, he wrote, 'I have sworn before a picture of the old and mourned comrade Stalin that I won't rest until I see these capitalist octopuses annihilated. In Guatemala I will perfect myself and achieve what I need to be an authentic revolutionary.'

The path to revolution was set. He took up arms and began waging war against imperialist powers, first in Cuba and then in other parts of the world. He was committed to his cause, and paid the ultimate price. He was assassinated in 1967 by order of the superpowers of his day, and buried anonymously with his hands cut off. His final words of defiance were, 'Shoot, coward, you're only going to kill a man.'

Guevara still remains an iconic figure. He fought for a better world through Marxism, but this ideology has not provided all the solutions. Cuba was his great victory and the country boasts free healthcare and schooling, but when I visited there I saw the fear with which people responded when I asked them about their lives. They were afraid of saying the wrong thing and incriminating the government. In Cuba there is only limited freedom of expression. Graffiti artist 'El Sexto' experienced this first-hand when he was imprisoned for ten months with no formal charge after painting the names of Raúl and Fidel (the first names of the Castro brothers who led the country) on the backs of two live pigs. Marxist ideals have come, but at a cost.

SIGNIFICANCE THROUGH CHANGE

The problem with the significance story is that when we gain what we have set out to achieve, we may find that things are still not right. We have failed to make the change that we want to make. If we seriously want to change the world and want significance to be our story, then we need to wrestle with some important questions. What is the right vision? What does a better world really look like? And how do we invest our lives accordingly? These questions are very difficult to answer because there is no one unifying story that helps us navigate our place in history.

We might choose to live out our lives like the young doctor Guevara, meeting the needs of those who have been marginalized and forgotten. But there will always be a sense that we are dealing with the consequences of a broken system. We will be challenged as to whether we should instead be investing our lives in challenging the corrupt systems that maintain such significant inequality.

Others might attempt to challenge the systems that leave the world so unequal. But how can we do this effectively? For some the answer might involve working within the systems that already exist. In the business sector, for example, capitalist entrepreneurs work to create jobs while sustainably caring for the planet and fostering community. Other people might approach this problem in a much more revolutionary manner, believing that banks and governments need to be toppled for a fairer system to be birthed. For them the ends justify the means; just as Guevara took up arms to conduct guerrilla warfare, some believe extreme action is needed.

However we wish to change the world, the reality is that it is complicated. More than just changing systems, ultimately we need to change human hearts. After the Iraq War during which Saddam Hussein was toppled, the USA launched a public relations campaign to reach the 'hearts and minds' of the Iraqi people. There was a realization that changing a nation is not simply about changing a government but about changing the people's perceptions – their hopes, their dreams, their stories.

Perhaps the issue with the significance story is best articulated by writer G. K. Chesterton, who about a century ago purportedly responded to an article in *The Times* that asked, 'What is wrong with the world today?' These were his words:

Dear Sirs:

I am.

Sincerely Yours,

G. K. Chesterton

Chesterton realized that ultimately each and every one of us is responsible for the mess the world is in. Revolution is often defined as sudden and dramatic change. Che Guevara brought revolution to Cuba. He brought it to a country but he failed to fully bring it to people's hearts. Martin Luther King helped achieve equal rights in the USA but racism today remains rife. Mother Teresa highlighted and cared for the poorest of the poor in Calcutta, but greed is still rampant. The root cause of corruption and inequality and violence is in you and me; it is in our human hearts.

So if we take the significance story seriously, we need to be the change we want to see, and that is extremely complex. We need to see the ways in which we are oppressors. We need to choose remorse. And we need to help change the hearts of others. A tall order but one that, as we will see later, takes a different shape if we choose to view the 'story of significance' through the lens of the 'God story'.

If we choose to live a story of significance as we try to change the world, we can easily become jaded as the complexity of issues becomes all too apparent. We can end up carrying the weight of our cause upon our shoulders, with our identity wrapped up in the limited change we can make. We may wonder if our life really is making a difference, and feel terribly insignificant. And somewhere deep inside we know this can't be right. We weren't made to live lives of insignificance.

WITHOUT A BIGGER STORY, WE LIVE FOR SMALL STORIES AND THESE SMALLER STORIES END UP DEFINING US.

Chapter five

A BIGGER STORY

In a sense, we are a very unusual society. We are trying to do something that no society has really done. We are trying to live without an agreed narrative of our communal place in the cosmos and in time.

Neil MacGregor

It had hung in the gallery for at least two years. Thousands had come to see it, to study it, to enjoy it. *Odalisque in Red Trousers*, one of Matisse's finest paintings, depicts a topless lady and is said to be worth around three million dollars. But little did the transfixed art critics know when they visited Venezuela's Caracas Museum of Contemporary Art that the painting was a fake. And not a very good fake at that.

It was not until a Miami-based art dealer informed the museum that he had been given the chance to buy the original painting that the staff realized that they had a fake hanging proudly on their wall. The museum had no idea exactly when the original Matisse had been taken and who had taken it. And it was some ten years before an FBI sting operation recovered the classic piece of art.

When it comes to finding a story for our lives, I believe there has been a theft. More than that, I believe we have been given fakes, and not very good ones at that.

It was the twentieth-century French philosopher Jean-François Lyotard who first coined the term 'meta-narrative'. Often translated as 'big story', it combines the Greek word *meta* meaning 'beyond, behind and transcendent' with 'narrative' meaning story.

Lyotard argued that in the present age we have lost the idea of meta-narratives – larger stories that frame our existence. Instead we have settled for smaller stories with ourselves at the epicentre. It's these smaller stories that I believe are the fakes. The story to be happy. The story to be safe. The story to be significant. We allow these stories to hang proudly over our lives, but the truth is, they are not big enough.

WHAT'S YOUR STORY?

The Camino de Santiago is an ancient pilgrimage route. The main path leads from the heights of the Pyrenees in France down into the vineyards of northern Spain and on to the ancient cathedral at Santiago de Compostela. During certain seasons of the year, the old route swells with throngs of people carrying their rucksacks trudging along dusty lanes via old monastic quarters. The mix of pilgrims, from different generations and different nations, embark on this epic journey knowing that it can take over two months to complete.

Each night, basic pilgrim hostels known as *auberges* offer accommodation and a hearty meal and there is time to meet your fellow travellers. Sharing freshly cooked pasta and goblets of wine, people share about why they are walking the Camino. Some do it for religious purposes; many are wanting to reassess their lives. They are taking time out, intentionally putting the career on hold so that they can grapple with what life is all about. Others may be going through a significant life transition – the divorce is finalized, they are graduating from university or are settling into retirement. The Camino provides time to re-evaluate what people want their lives to be about.

I'd always been intrigued by the famous pilgrimage and agreed to join my mum for a section of the route, taking time out myself to discern the next part of my life story. With this host of people to share life with each evening, strangers quickly became friends. I loved asking, 'So, what's your story?' It's the kind of question that is so open-ended it can sometimes flummox people. But this question acts as a diving board into a stranger's life. The responder can choose where to start, what to include and where to finish. There is an opportunity to share successes and regrets, hopes and fears.

In a strong Irish accent, one man explained that he was walking the Camino because his wife had just died and he was struggling to determine the next part of his story. He shared about meeting his wife for the first time as a young man. The romance and the proposal. Raising a family with her. The children, the happy memories, their life together. And then he shared about the life-sucking disease that had eaten away at her as he nursed her through her terminal illness. He shared about the funeral. About grief. About coming to terms with loss.

Stories frame our experiences and I found that as people shared the narrative of their life so far they meticulously wove together distinct moments and instances into one linear story. Telling their story helped them to begin to make sense of what they had experienced and also gave clues about their deeply held beliefs. And it's when we begin to talk about our life in terms of a story that we discover that we are in fact building upon a much bigger story. A story we often refer to as faith.

THIS THING CALLED FAITH

Faith is a funny word. It sounds like a very religious term that we associate with those who are superstitious or identify with a particular religious group. We tend to think of priests, monks and overzealous individuals. But the truth is, we all have faith. Faith is fundamentally our explanation for why we are here. It is the story of our existence.

Some believe that the world is just about what we can see. Our explanation is that there was a Big Bang and somehow, by chance, the world was created. There is no creator or masterplan. We come from dust and we go back to dust. That is it. This is our explanation and we live accordingly.

For others of us, as we live out our lives, there is something that suggests there is more to life than what we can understand in a laboratory. There is mystery. We have had spiritual experiences, good or bad, that just can't be shaken off. We look for something to help us live life well and deal with the reality of death. This is equally our explanation and so we live accordingly.

This thing called faith – our explanation for why we are here – profoundly affects how we see the world and how we create a story for our lives. But it can often feel very wishy-washy. It can seem as if we're unplugging our brains and jumping into the unknown. But we all have faith and it is built upon the evidence that surrounds us. In the same way in which we sew together moments from our lives to communicate a linear story, so we weave together our experiences, our education and our understanding to try to comprehend why we are here in the first place.

★

Children are inquisitive. They look at the world from a unique perspective. It's in having my own family that my curiosity has been sparked again and again over things that I would rarely give a moment's thought to. As children look at the world, they continually ask the question, 'Why?'

Walking to nursery, our amble along the road is interrupted by a line of ants walking rhythmically across the pavement and up a tree carrying leaves. 'What are they doing, Daddy? How can ants climb trees? Do ants talk? What do ants eat?' A barrage of questions from an inquisitive three-year-old sees me quickly retrieve my phone from my pocket and start googling.

Science is this innate desire to understand the world around us. It comes from the Latin *scio*, to know. And having children has meant studying the planets at night, checking out dinosaur fossils, watching wildlife programmes and examining ants navigating their way up a tree. It has drawn me back into the wonder of creation.

As we grow older, we can become less inquisitive. We may think we have enough evidence for the explanation we have adopted and it never occurs to us to challenge it. Whether we have grown up in religious homes or have a materialistic background, we often stick to the framework or explanation we have been given without ever asking questions.

With our views set in concrete, we look around the world instinctively interpreting what we see to make sense of them. Too often we don't give things a second thought. If we believe that nothing is spiritual, when someone talks about answered prayer we think it's just coincidence. If we believe that everything is spiritual, when someone talks about a vivid dream they've had we might immediately read some deep meaning into it, rather than just asking how much cheese they ate before heading to bed. We tend to operate on default.

Questions are important in reassessing why we believe what we believe. But the important thing to recognize here is that faith is not about certainty. Faith is built from our interpretation of the evidence we have to hand.

NOTHING IS CERTAIN

It was a cold night as I got down on to bended knee in the main square in Tallinn, Estonia. I pulled out the plastic make-do ring and asked my girlfriend to marry me. I had never been so nervous and the words tumbled out of my mouth more in a stream of unconsciousness than a thought-through marriage proposal. Her response? She began to cry.

Now I'm not always great at discerning happy tears from sad tears but it turned out they were the happy ones and she accepted. With the figures around divorce rates, I had been rather reticent about the idea of marriage. There is no certainty, no guarantee that things will work out. But I knew I wanted to be married to Jo. I had a deep-seated confidence that I wanted to spend the rest of my life with her. We share similar visions for our lives. We had already journeyed through highs and lows together. She was for me and I was for her. She understood me and I felt I understood her. It was this deep-seated confidence that enabled me to take out the ring on bended knee.

We don't enter marriage with certainty but we must enter it with a confidence – confidence that is built on the evidence we have that our relationship can go the distance. It's the same with faith.

★

We had just hiked up a particularly gruelling peak of the Camino when I came across a Hungarian man in his mid-thirties. He had been trekking for three days. As we momentarily stopped to catch our breath, he shared how that morning he had made a detour to the post office. He had discovered that he had way too much in his rucksack, including some things that were non-essential and were wearing him down. That morning he had sent half the contents of his bag back home because they were just not necessary. And today, walking had suddenly become significantly easier.

Our faith story, our explanation for why we are here, can too easily be made up of excess baggage – things we have never really challenged but continue to make an impact on the story we are living today. We can be weighed down by our faith story rather than liberated to live life well. Because faith always becomes action.

My old red Skoda, sold to me by my salesman brother, had a number of particular quirks. Perhaps the most random was the fact that to turn the radio on I needed to lean over and open the passenger door while driving. Its final journey ended abruptly with smoke pouring from the bonnet at 3 a.m. on an empty road in the middle of France.

But the day we took off on our French adventure, I had complete faith in the old banger. I know very little about cars but I realize that every time I strap myself in and start the engine, I am putting an enormous amount of faith into many contraptions. I am trusting that the steering wheel works, that the gears will shift up and down as I ask them to, that the brakes will be effective and that my seat belt will protect me if I am involved in a collision. Having driven many cars over the years, I have faith that cars work and are generally safe, and this faith is demonstrated every time I turn on the ignition.

It's easy to say that we believe something, but our actions reveal what we really believe. They reveal the faith story that underpins everything else. It makes no sense for someone who argues that everything is material to pray. In the same way, it makes no sense for someone who argues that there is more than the material world to base every decision solely on what can be seen.

★

In a country where there had been much persecution of Christians, a group gathered together to worship in a church building one Sunday morning. Voices of all ages filled the small building with singing but then there was suddenly a crashing interruption as armed militia burst into the service. The militia, aiming guns at the Christians, told the stunned worshippers that they had two minutes to recant their faith and leave the building, or they would be assassinated. There were tears as some people left while others stayed. Parents said goodbye to their children, children said goodbye to their parents, as the gravity of the situation struck home.

The militia cocked their guns and told the worshippers they had ten seconds left. A few more fled the building, until only a handful of Christians remained. At this point the militia put down their weapons and explained that they too wanted to become Christians, but they wanted to hear about the Christian faith from those who really believed it. Faith has to be about action, otherwise it isn't really faith at all.

Finding our story provokes us to go beyond the superficial. We need first to unearth our faith story, like buried treasure, and look at it from a fresh perspective. And as we do this, we need to remember that faith is never certainty. None of us can be certain that our explanation of why we are here is 100 per cent correct. Instead it is about this deep-seated confidence on which we build our life story.

Some people systematically work through different belief systems, carefully weighing up evidence, but the majority of us don't approach life in this way. We don't give much thought to why we believe what we believe. We don't make the effort to explore the faith story that underpins our lives. Perhaps more of us should take time out to reflect on what we believe, to hear other people's stories, to let them make an impact on our own.

And so things are often not clear cut. We are not fully sure why we are here. We have a confidence in one worldview one minute and another the next. Sometimes what we do suggests that we believe everything is material, at other times we act as though there is more than meets the eye. They say that when a plane is about to crash, there are no atheists.

With a rich melting pot of philosophies and religions at our disposal, many of us have a faith that has little consistency. So we settle for the three common motifs that appear to make most sense: happiness, safety and significance. As great as aspects of each of these stories may be, I believe there is a faith story that stands the test of time, one that I have found a deep-seated confidence in. As I mentioned earlier, I don't think we were ever meant to be the centre of the story. I believe there's an original masterpiece – a meta-narrative, in Lyotard's term – that needs to be explored. Do I have all the answers? No. But this big narrative has helped me and continues to help me find my story.

As much as I love science, it can too often reduce everything to the lowest common denominator. I believe we are more than just a complicated concoction of chemicals. I believe love is more than just a series of chemical reactions. And I believe life has purpose. Without a bigger story, we are left believing that what we do is not important; how we live is not important. We live for small stories and these smaller stories end up defining us. The truth is, happiness can never be measured and utopia is not possible. Fear means building bigger walls but we can never really escape the uncertainty of life. And the search for significance can be all about us and can become an unbearably heavy burden to carry. As stories, they may look like the real deal, but in fact they end up reminding us that we are just a collection of molecules defined by our emotions, our bank balance or the limited impact for good that we can make.

And so let me tell you a story – one that I believe is the most compelling story of all. A story that spans human history and has inspired generations of ordinary people to live life well. It may be the first time you have heard it; or you may have heard it many times before but need to hear again. Let's step into the God story . . .

THE BOOKENDS OF A STORY ARE VITALLY IMPORTANT. WHERE A STORY BEGINS AND WHERE A STORY ENDS FRAME THE NARRATIVE.

Chapter six

THE GOD STORY

In the end science does not provide the answers most of us require. The story of our origins and our end is, to say the least, unsatisfactory. To the question 'how did it all begin?' science answers, 'probably by accident' and to the question 'how will it all end?' science answers, 'probably by accident'. And to many people the accidental life is not worth living.

Neil Postman

The bookends of a story are vitally important. Where a story begins and where a story ends frame the narrative. The God story that we find in the Bible begins with God and ends with God and his people. It begins with God creating everything. He creates the heavens and the earth, bringing order out of chaos. What is formless and empty and dark becomes this stunning creation, full of life and colour.

First, there is light. Then he creates the sky and separates land and water. Golden beaches and beautiful cliffs and glistening lakes and deep blue skies and spectacular mountains and turquoise oceans.

Then come plants and trees and vegetation. Great oak trees, stunning cherry blossom, palm trees, Venus flytraps, waterlilies, delicate dandelions and creamy flowering hawthorn.

There follow the sun and moon and stars. Sunsets and full moons, eclipses and meteors that dance through the night sky. And then there are animals. Crocodiles and parrots and armadillos and dragonflies and elephants and beavers and octopuses and sting-rays.

It's in the opening words of this story in Genesis, the first book of the Bible, that we meet God. The main character is not you or me but God. A God who creates beauty. And from kick-off, there is the revelation that God is Love. He refers to himself as 'us' – the concept that he is three in one (Genesis 1.26). Some theologians call this the divine dance that reveals the loving relationship at the very core of who God is.

This opening sequence is so rich. Too often the creation story has become an argument about how literally the events should be taken, rather than an opportunity to stop in wonder at the very character of God who creates everything. From him, everything exists.

And then he creates humanity in 'our image' (Genesis 1.26). We are set apart from the rest of creation, possessing a relational and creative capacity like God. In this beautiful intimate picture, God takes Adam, whose name means earthling, whom he has created from the dust, and breathes life into his lungs (Genesis 2.7). God gives the breath of life to humanity.

Throughout this opening to the story the recurring word is 'good'. Again and again, what has been created is good. Everything is good. But then there is a jarring as Adam, created alone, is not good in himself (Genesis 2.18). And so God creates woman, a companion. This does not mean that every man needs a woman to be complete (or vice versa), but demonstrates that we were created to be in relationship rather than individual islands, to share life and adventure and stories together. As such, we are the pinnacle of God's creation.

This phenomenal opening sequence, set in a stunning garden brimming with life and colour, continues as God chooses to be in partnership with humanity, with you and me. He calls on us to serve and preserve creation (Genesis 1.28); this story is not a finished picture but an unfolding piece of artistry in which we are invited to join with God.

Nothing is static. Everything is filled with potential. The vegetation is full of seeds for the future, animals are given the ability to procreate, the sun and moon give rhythm and seasons to what lies ahead and man and woman are given the command to multiply. It's like a pull-back toy car, full of energy, suddenly being released to race forward across the living-room carpet. The future is full of exciting possibilities. There is order. There is harmony. Everything fits together.

This story has so much depth to it. It shows us that we are not a cosmic accident, and just happen to exist. We are created with intent. We have purpose, as God invites us into his unfolding story. As mentioned earlier, every good story has a character who wants something. And from the very beginning, it is clear that God wants us. He wants you and me to be in relationship with him. He wants intimacy and harmony and partnership. This is where the real story begins.

The God story in the pages of the Bible starts in a garden and ends in a city. There was always going to be this progression in the story. The choice of humanity to put itself front and centre in the story, usurping God, has meant that the journey has become ever more convoluted. But the story ends with God getting what he wants. His kingdom arrives. There is a new heaven and a new earth; the biblical word used here for new isn't *neos* meaning 'brand new' but *kainos* meaning 'renewed' (Revelation 21.1). The story is not about escaping planet Earth but about God redeeming his perfect creation. God renews all things.

This future reality beckons us. The book of Revelation, a prophetic vision of the end of the story, tells of a city where God dwells among his people, where he washes away every tear. God gets what he wants. He gets to live in proximity to his people who recognize that he is the very centrepiece of history (Revelation 22.1–5).

From paradise lost to paradise gained; from creation to a picture of restoration. Because of this, there is always hope as we live between the bookends. The story begins in a perfect garden and ends with a perfect city. But the story is not straightforward. Rather than moving on seamlessly, there is a dramatic twist in the tale.

FAULT LINE

With the creation story complete, we begin to imagine God's heartache as a fault line appears (Genesis 3). Just a few hundred words into the narrative, we have the powerful moment when God, walking in the cool of the day, calls out to humanity, 'Where are you?'

Adam and Eve have hidden. They have broken his one command. Tricked by a serpent, they ate from the tree of good and evil and immediately realized that they were naked. And so they have hidden. But there is no hiding from the consequences of their decision, and no hiding from God. Their decision has immediate implications.

Every time I read this story I think, why? Life was good. They were able to walk with God. They were living in harmony. They were partnering with the Creator. Why did they choose to go against this one simple command? The Genesis story tells us that they thought they could 'be like God, knowing good and evil'. In essence they wanted to take God's role. They wanted to take control, to be the very centre of the story. And then I realize that often I, just like them, have made myself the centre of the story.

And it's in this moment of humanity's disobedience that everything is thrown out of sync. Everything changes. What is good has been corrupted. A spiritual battle kicks off as humanity neglects its responsibility and death enters the picture. Most evidently, our relationship with God is broken. A God who is holy, who is perfect, cannot be in a daily relationship with an imperfect humanity. Adam and Eve are banished from the garden, and this broken relationship is systemic, corrupting our relationship with everything else and spelling out death.

There is disorder. There is chaos. Everything is broken.

It's not just our relationship with God that is broken but our relationship with one another. By the next generation there is murder in the family; within a few more generations stories of rape and greed and violence and hatred are rife. Humanity is broken.

Our relationship with creation is also in tatters. The beauty that God created is corrupted, the spiritual fallout of that one decision to eat from the forbidden tree is realized in floods and earthquakes and hurricanes and diseases and endless carnage. Creation can no longer fully reflect the beauty and the glory of God.

And finally, our relationship with ourselves is distorted. We become defined by place and by family; by our past and by our vision for the future; by our brokenness and by our togetherness; by our failings and by our accomplishments. But no longer by how God sees us.

At this point it becomes clear that God wants something. The pages of the Bible take us on a journey through the unfolding God story – God on a mission to restore broken relationships. There are kings and empires and conspiracies and battles. Relationships consistently come to grief. But behind it all there is God. He longs to deal with the consequences of Adam and Eve's decision in the garden. He longs for things to be put right. And the stories in the Old Testament show time and time again how this was not possible.

The story of Noah and his family, who were rescued from a great flood along with two of each kind of animal, shows us that things were not made right even by flooding the earth and starting again (Genesis 7). In the story of Israel, God raised a nation he was committed to lead; they were blessed to be a blessing, to represent God's character, but this ultimately ended in failure. The stories of countless judges and prophets and kings and priests could not bring people back into relationship with God by calling them to account.

There was a problem at the very core of humanity that had to be dealt with. The human heart needed to be changed. There was only one option left. And so begins the next chapter of the God story.

EMMANUEL

God so wants intimacy and harmony and partnership that the three-in-one God sends himself; he sends Jesus. He is the only way things can be put right. God becomes flesh. Jesus is Emmanuel, God with us (John 1).

Holding my daughter's first pink stripy Babygro is a powerful reminder of how small she once was. It's mind-blowing to think how much she has grown, and more so to think that I once used to fill one of these tiny outfits myself. Even more astonishing is that God enters humanity as a baby.

The Jesus story is fascinating. Not born into a palace but into poverty, he becomes the child of an unmarried couple; at his birth there are irreligious shepherds and stargazers who were not from God's chosen nation, Israel. The Son of God is surrounded by those you least expect. His early years are spent as the son of a carpenter; he flees as a refugee to Egypt and grows up in Nazareth, the armpit of Israel, under the dominance of the Roman Empire.

But somehow, with all the cards stacked against him, Jesus changes the face of human history. He waits until he is 30 before his ministry goes public, and from there it takes just three years to kick-start a movement. It begins with a random collection of all sorts of people, a jumbled assortment of characters: revolutionaries, Roman sympathizers, simple fishermen and well-off tax collectors. And for those three years he invites them to travel around Israel with him.

John, one of his twelve closest followers, in his account of the life of Jesus makes it clear that Jesus is claiming that when people see him they see the very character of God (John 14.9). As Jesus travels he demonstrates God's power, healing the sick and raising the dead. He also demonstrates God's anger as he challenges the religious elite and threatens the corrupt status quo. And as he travels he demonstrates God's compassion, welcoming the outcast and restoring human dignity. Jesus lives his life according to God's story.

In among all this action, Jesus tells stories of his own. He was probably the greatest storyteller that ever lived. His stories drew thousands of listeners at once, stories that showed that another world was possible. They made the comfortable feel uncomfortable, while comforting the uncomfortable.

Jesus understood the power of story. And as we read these ancient stories of what Jesus said and did we get powerful insights into the very heart of God.

One day Jesus turns up at the house of his friend Lazarus (John 11.38–44). Three days earlier Lazarus had died. The scene must have been chaotic with people wailing and grieving. Jesus is about to bring Lazarus back to life; but before he does this momentous miracle, he stops and weeps. Jesus weeps. Why? I think that in that moment Jesus witnesses, from a human perspective, the reality of grief. With the story that begins in Genesis, we can be sure that this was never how things were meant to be. Death was never intended to be part of the story. So not only do we get these insights into the heart of God, we get insights into what it really means to be human. Jesus, as fully God and fully man, models how we should live.

Among all the action of miracles, controversy and storytelling, Jesus continually punctuated his day with space, with quiet, with aloneness with his Father. When Jesus heals a cripple on the holy day, the sabbath, the religious leaders get vexed and confront him, asking why he has done such a thing. Jesus responds that he is simply doing 'what he sees his Father doing' (John 5.19). Jesus shows us what it looks like to be defined not by expectations, by his followers, his spectacular miracles or religious presumptions, but by his relationship with the Father. Jesus' life shows us the simplicity and at times the difficulty in finding our humanity in our relationship with the Father in heaven, not by what we do.

Then comes another garden and another choice. In the Garden of Gethsemane Jesus begs his friends to keep watch as he spends time in prayer. But his closest friends, who have witnessed him do so much, can't stay awake (Luke 22). And it's in this garden that Jesus wrestles with the decision to go to the cross. The decision is so intense that he sweats blood. Adam and Eve chose selfishness in a garden; here in a different garden Jesus chooses selflessness. As the arresting party move in, their lanterns dancing through the night sky, Jesus makes no attempt to escape. His disciples flee but he is willingly arrested, knowing he is innocent.

And the next day Jesus is crucified on a cross. The most horrendous and bloody of executions possible. And we call that day Good Friday. It's a strange name for the day on which Jesus was crucified. Pierced hands and feet. A crown of thorns. A spear in his side. Good?

But it is a good day because on this day God gets what he wants. Jesus agonizingly cries out, 'It is finished.' As he does so his perfect selfless act deals with our imperfect selfish acts and opens up a way for intimacy and harmony and partnership (John 19.30). Evil is defeated. This is how much God wants us. Good Friday is the ultimate expression of generosity. God's character becomes fully evident. His justice meant that he was unable to let things stay as they were, and his love allowed the innocent life of his son Jesus to pay my debt and pay yours.

For three days it looked as if the God story had failed. Game over. It appeared that Jesus had been snuffed out by the superpower of the day. His closest friends had deserted him. But then comes the twist. It was the first day of the new week, but really it was the first day of a new creation. As women go to visit the grave with spices, they discover that the tomb is empty. Jesus has conquered death. This was not the end; it was really a new chapter.

THE NOW AND THE NOT YET

After his resurrection Jesus meets with his disciples. He meets the same people, in the same room, in the same city, but everything is different. Jesus has defeated death and God's narrative is taking shape. Jesus now has a resurrection body and he calls his ordinary ragtag group of followers to change the world. They are commissioned to make disciples as the Holy Spirit fills them, leads them and empowers them to share the good news that nobody need live with broken relationships any more, that everyone can have intimacy and harmony and partnership with God (Matthew 28).

And almost 2,000 years on, we too have the opportunity to become part of God's story. Jesus set in motion a movement, a community, called the Church. We become the hands and feet of Jesus, sharing his love and truth with a broken and hurting world. This is our subplot story. And right now we live between the bookends. We live in a now and we live in a not yet. In the now, we live with the death-conquering reality of Jesus' death and resurrection. We live with the reality of intimacy with God, the reality of beginning to live in harmony as his people. We live in the reality of being supernaturally empowered by his Spirit to partner in seeing what God wants established on earth. The New Testament writers refer to this as the kingdom of God – a reality where God gets what he wants, things are as they should be and we live with a deep sense of peace.

But we also live in the not yet. Things are not fully as they should be. We still have a distorted understanding of our value. There are still warring nations, broken relationships and natural disasters. In fact Paul, one of the writers of the New Testament, articulates that creation is groaning and yearning for the not yet. The kingdom is not fully here (Romans 8). Jesus' death and resurrection established him as King, but we wait for his return when his kingdom will become a known reality for everyone and everything.

And so this is where we find ourselves, between the beginning and the end of the narrative. We have this amazing hope ahead but live in the reality of today. The Church is the vehicle for God's story of grace and truth to be shown to the world. And we are invited to play our part.

THIS WAS A STORY
THAT COULD FRAME
ALL OUR STORIES,
PROMISING THAT WE
HAD SOME SENSE
OF VALUE AND
PURPOSE AND THAT
NO MATTER WHAT WE
ENCOUNTERED, THERE
WAS ALWAYS HOPE.

Chapter seven

MY STORY

Neither revolution nor reformation can ultimately change a society, rather you must tell a new powerful tale, one so persuasive that it sweeps away the old myths and becomes the preferred story, one so inclusive that it gathers all the bits of our past and our present into a coherent whole, one that even shines some light into the future so that we can take the next step ... if you want to change a society then you have to tell an alternative story.

Ivan Illich

It was 1 October 1971. The grand opening of Disney World in Florida. Five years earlier Walt Disney had died, and during the dedication ceremony someone turned to Mrs Disney and said, 'Isn't it a shame that Walt didn't live to see this?' Mrs Disney's reply? 'He did see it, that's why it's here.'

Walt Disney was a man of vision who knew what made a good story. He is known for his characters, his movies and his theme parks. But Walt Disney is also known in certain circles for his strategic gift – his immense ability to turn creative ideas into reality. One of Disney's associates would say, 'There were actually three different Walts: the dreamer, the realist and the spoiler. You never knew which one was coming to the meeting.' He had the ability to dream, to explore practicalities, and also the ability to 'spoil' – to challenge, critique, find holes in the initial idea.

Disney's method has been turned into a strategy used by teams in all kinds of industries for turning dreams into reality. It involves creating three rooms. Room One is the Dream Room. This room is open and airy with a high ceiling and lots of light. Participants sit in a circle and are encouraged to collaborate and create as they dream about what could be. Imagination is allowed to run riot. Room Two is the Reality Room. This is a practical space with a large whiteboard for strategic planning. In this realist phase concepts are worked out in the nitty-gritty; it is all about constructing together. In this room dreams are turned from imaginary ideas into a manageable action plan. Then there is Room Three, the Spoiler Room. A smaller, more constrained space with a single row of chairs facing the action plan, the room promotes criticism of the project in order to find the barriers, the weak points, the hidden traps. Only having been through this rhythm of rooms several times is a concept agreed on.

It's interesting to examine our life story by moving metaphorically through Walt's three rooms: dreaming, realizing and critiquing. As we do this, we begin to see the connection between our deep-lying explanation of why we are here and the story we have for our lives.

TEENAGE EXPLORATION

By my teenage years I had pretty much rejected the God story. I had been brought up in a Christian home and subconsciously I had used Walt's three rooms to work out that this was not for me. If the first room is about dreaming then I had decided that the God story was not the dream for my life. The God story had never really bitten. Growing up in the church, singing hymns that made no sense and the archaic language of kingdom, coupled with the obscurity of what that looked like, meant that the vision proposed in the pages of the Bible had not inspired me. This was not a dream that excited me. It had never captured my imagination.

In the second room, when we get real and visualize, I had begun to explore what the story meant practically for my life, and as I did so I was sure it wasn't a fit. I wanted a life of adventure and excitement. I didn't want to live a dull and boring half-life, stuck in church meetings. And then with the spoiler room, there seemed to be just too many holes in the God story for it to be true. My friends who were adamant atheists used to love challenging the Bible and all it stood for.

So by the time I was 18 I had decided that the God story was not for me. I didn't need to take some ancient version of a Disney fairytale to be the framework for living my life. But now, 20 years on, the God story is central to working out how I live out my story, because at that moment, when I was 18, something happened.

RE-ENTERING THE DREAM ROOM

That year, when I was on the brink of adulthood, I applied to work on a summer camp in the USA. I filled in my application form knowing that I could be positioned anywhere in the country. To help find me a suitable camp, the form involved a long list of tick boxes. Each item was something that I might be able to teach to American young people. I could teach football and drama and archery so I ticked those; and as I scanned this list, I saw that one of the boxes read Bible stories. And so, to give myself the optimum chance of being selected, I ticked that box too.

When I landed in Seattle I discovered that I was going to be working in a Salvation Army camp, working with young people from gangs. And it was on my way to the camp that I found out that they were expecting me to teach the Bible to some of these kids – kids with gang tattoos, stab scars and bullet wounds . . .

I have to admit that I felt completely out of my depth. I had rejected the God story for myself and yet I was being asked to share this narrative with gang members just a couple of years younger than me. I began to imagine the absurdity of becoming a martyr for something I didn't even believe in. Too embarrassed to inform the camp of my true feelings, I decided to give it a shot. And during that summer something happened. I discovered that as I shared stories from the Bible I could see how these disen-franchised young people were encountering something of God. I saw them discover forgiveness and thankfulness and a story for their lives.

Redemption is a very religious-sounding word but in essence it means to buy back. At the heart of the Christian story God, through the life, death and resurrection of Jesus, pays the necessary cost to restore all things. It's in this old word that we discover the heart of the God story. Many of the young people I worked with that summer had been written off and yet the God story insists that we all have worth and value and that a better world is possible. During those weeks I saw the beauty of the God story, and that this was a story that could frame all our stories, promising that we had some sense of value and purpose and that no matter what we encountered, there was always hope.

GETTING REAL

It's in the middle room that we get real. We put legs on a concept and see if it can walk. In my early teens I found church services exceptionally boring. This was not how I wanted to spend my Sunday mornings. Somewhere along the line I began to visualize my story as a Christian as living a life tempered by a rule book written almost 2,000 years ago. I believed that being a Christian meant living a constrained life, with lists of things I couldn't do.

But during that summer camp my perceptions were changed. I discovered that the God story was not about limiting what I could do but about freeing me to live a better story. And I discovered the role I could play in seeing lives changed. From that point on, as I have tried to live my life as part of this bigger story, I have found that the Christian faith is not about living a safe and predictable life. Instead it's about encountering a God who created us, who designed us and who knows just what we need.

★

Jack grew up in Belfast in the early twentieth century. He was brought up in a devout home but at the age of ten his mum died and he was sent off to boarding school. He became disillusioned with the Christian faith in his youth and he turned his back on the Christian story.

At Oxford University he joined a group of writers and intellectuals called The Inklings. Through conversations with this group Jack rather reluctantly came to believe the story found in the Bible and recommitted himself to God. He wrote, 'I have found a desire within myself that no experience in this world can satisfy; the most probable explanation is that I was made for another world.' Better known as C. S. Lewis, Jack went on to be one of the best story writers of all time, penning the Narnia Chronicles. He argued that we all have needs that are only met in the God who created us.

The website PostSecret is a community art project where people send in their secrets anonymously on postcards. Some of them are quite funny, such as: 'Sometimes I go to the toilet just to get some peace and quiet', and 'I still write to Father Christmas. I am 17 and Jewish'. But some are darker confessions: 'I wish you would stop being so concerned about my weight and be more concerned about by lack of happiness', and 'I sometimes beat myself black and blue, just to feel something'. There are confessions about abuse, about regrets and about failed relationships.

There is a profound need in all of us to be heard. And we have a need to confess, to get things off our chest, to be in some way forgiven and accepted. As I read some of these postcards my heart becomes heavy. They are from people I have never met and will probably never know. They may live in a different corner of the planet, yet these postcards, which represent their story, are heartbreaking.

You see, wrapped up in my humanity is a desire for justice. We each carry a sense of what is right and wrong, a sense of morality. And when we hear stories about injustice in the world, where people are trafficked or abused, we can get really angry, even when these people may be in some distant land and their stories may never impinge upon our lives.

We might not believe in a Creator, yet we have inbuilt needs and desires – for forgiveness, for justice. We are aware of other needs too: the need to thank someone for the amazing sunset that sets the sky ablaze, or to be able to express ourselves creatively. Or perhaps ultimately the need to find a story for our lives.

It's these needs that I think C. S. Lewis was talking about. The Christian story is about discovering that we have a Creator, who made us in his image. He does not want to be distant but wants to be with us. In the good times and in the painful times. And as I have thrown in my lot with this story I have begun to see the reality of my life as part of God's story. I have discovered that it's not about living by a series of rules but about having a relationship where God nourishes and provokes and leads. It's not always easy. In fact, at times it's hard. But I have also discovered, time and time again, that when my story is wrapped in his, life is anything but boring.

SPOILER ALERT

Far from the adventure-free life I feared God would have for me, I've had the privilege of travelling extensively. In exploring distant lands I am always amazed by the diversity of planet Earth. From the rich green canopy of the rainforest, alive with sounds of weird-looking creatures, to the windswept mountains of sand in the desert that contrast powerfully with the piercing blue skies, the planet we call home is breathtaking. Even within my grey corner of London the trees blossom in the spring with the most brilliant of pinks, and the autumnal hues are richer in colour than any artist's painting.

On the all too rare occasions when I bring my wife flowers, I see her face light up. The thought behind the giving of flowers matters, but often it's a very random act. Living in our clean, sterilized homes, it may seem strange to bring in something from the garden and put it in pride of place. But thankfully my wife never finds it strange – there is something intrinsically beautiful and stunning and good about flowers. Creation is good.

One of my favourite places to enjoy creation is the ocean. Surfing up and down head-high walls of water breaking around a rocky headland sends adrenaline pumping around my body. As I clamber out of the water, people often come and make conversation, bemused by the seal-like creatures braving the wintry waters. They commonly ask, 'Do you not need wind for the waves?'

There is this presumption that a windy day is good for surfing. In fact, surfers generally prefer either no wind at all or perhaps a gentle offshore breeze. The preferred waves for surfers are caused not by howling winds along the coastline nearby but by storms hundreds of miles away. These low pressure weather patterns in a distant part of the world send ripples across the ocean that finally arrive on a beach for surfers to take advantage of.

It's as you get into an activity like surfing that you begin to comprehend the complexity of your experience and how it is affected by weather systems, wave energy and sandbank formations. Surfing might not be your forte. If you are into fine cuisine, for example, you will be aware of the complexity of taste. The mouth contains between 6,000 and 8,000 taste buds that detect salty, sour, sweet and savoury tastes. And if you enjoy gazing at the night sky, you're probably aware that the light from the stars we see has taken four years to reach your retina.

In my teens I heard a lot of critiques of the Bible, but today I find that the story we find in it makes more sense than any other. For me, there is no way that this creation could have come about by chance. Creation shows me that there is a Creator, and its complexity and intricacy point to a depth of design that is unparalleled.

When I talk about creation as evidence for God, people often point out, 'But what about the brokenness of creation?' I understand what they mean. When a friend is diagnosed with a serious form of cancer, or when I see on the news that a cyclone has ripped through an island in the Caribbean that is already struggling, something deep inside me cries out that this not fair. This is not the way things should be.

For me, it's not only about the beauty and the complexity of creation. The brokenness of creation affirms the story that we find in the Bible. It's God's story that makes sense of the world and I believe this ancient book was inspired by God and has the power to speak into our lives today.

★

Standing at 309.7 metres, the Shard towers over the London skyline, its 11,000 panes of glass reflecting the sky above. Its appearance changes with the weather. Inspired by railway lines, church steeples and the masts of sailing ships that would have travelled down the Thames, the building is presently the tallest in Western Europe. When you ask the question, 'Who built the Shard?', the answer you get is Renzo Piano. He was the award-winning designer and architect. But did he dig the foundations and craft the iron and fix in place any of the panes of glass? No.

The Bible used to baffle me when I was young. It was described as the Word of God but this would confuse me further. The Bible is not an easy book to get a handle on, mainly because it isn't just one book, but a library of books written in different genres, in different cultures, by different authors, over thousands of years. Rather than simply being a blueprint for life or a list of rules and regulations, the Bible gives us a story that reveals the character of God.

And although the Bible has many authors, I believe there is ultimately one author – God. But just as Renzo Piano didn't put in any window panes, God didn't dictate the words of the Bible;

he inspired authors to write an account of their revelation. It's an unfolding drama, stuffed full of stories, and the overarching designer and architect is God. That is why we refer to it as the Word of God. It's as I have studied and reflected upon the stories found in the Bible that I have become more and more convinced of the authenticity of this book. It is particularly the story of Jesus that grips me.

It's easy to critique a book you haven't read and many dismiss the Bible in this way. But in the teaching of Jesus we find otherworldly wisdom. His teaching remains relevant today, forming the basis of many of our Western values. The simplicity of 'loving your neighbour as you love yourself' is a case in point. And interestingly the teaching of Jesus speaks directly into the three common stories we often live for in the Western world, namely happiness, staying safe and the desire for significance.

With thousands clamouring to hear his stories, Jesus is interrupted while speaking to them with a question about monetary inheritance. And Jesus says that life is not defined by what you have, even when you have a lot (Luke 12.15). Jesus then explains this truth by telling a story about a rich man who owned farmland. He had a bumper harvest and found that his barns were not big enough to store the crops. So he tore down his barns and built bigger ones. He gathered in his crops, and thought he'd done well, that he had finally made it. Now he could kick back and have the time of his life. But that night, God shows up and says, 'You fool! Tonight you will die. And your barns full of goods – who gets them now?' (Luke 12.20).

The rich man was thinking that he was about to live the good life now he was rich. He was probably feeling safe and secure, with barns stacked full. And perhaps he felt particularly significant with the power that stemmed from his wealth. He may have been living for all of the three stories we live by, as might many of Jesus' listeners, but as the story ends it shows the futility of these narratives. Jesus finishes with a killer line, 'That's what happens when you fill your barn with self and not with God.' It's almost as if Jesus drops the microphone and walks off stage.

But, you might be thinking, there have been many other wise gurus throughout history – Plato, Socrates, Aristotle. But for me it's not just about the unmatched stories and wisdom of Jesus, it's about his very life, death and resurrection.

★

Lee was a lawyer by background. He was the legal editor for the *Chicago Tribune* and an adamant atheist. So he was very shocked the day his wife came home and told him that she had become a Christian. The first two words to enter his mind were an expletive and 'divorce'.

He became fixated on disproving Christianity to his wife. As he began to read the Bible, he surmised that the whole Christian faith rested upon the resurrection of Jesus. If Jesus had not risen from the dead, then the whole Christian faith could be dismantled. With his legal background, he began detailed research into the resurrection. He writes, 'In the end, after I had thoroughly investigated the matter, I reached an unexpected conclusion: it would actually take more faith to maintain my atheism than to become a follower of Jesus.' Lee Strobel has now been a Christian for 30 years.

The simple truth is that when we enter the Spoiler Room, the God story has stood the test of time. The God story is believable.

THE DISNEY EMPIRE

Around 20 million people every year visit what was thousands of acres of marshland at the intersection of a couple of freeways in Florida. Disneyland continues to be the most visited theme park in the world. It's clear that Walt Disney had the power to dream. But more than just the ability to dream, Walt was both a realist and a spoiler. His dream was grounded in practicality and he had done the hard work of critiquing it first.

In my teenage years I had written off the God story, but that summer when I was 18 I saw the beauty of the Christian story. I have chosen to put my faith in the author of that story – God. Over the years I have revisited those three rooms metaphorically on various occasions. I have spent time in the Dream Room, becoming more deeply familiar with God's story. I have spent time in the Reality Room, exploring both the adventure and the cost of living in this story. And I have spent time the Spoiler Room, working through people's questions and challenges. I don't want to believe some wishy-washy fairytale.

But each time I emerge from these three rooms, I believe that the God story makes sense. Over the centuries empires have come and gone. One day even the Disney empire will be just a relic of history. But the God story has lasted 2,000 years and I have such a deep-seated confidence in this story that I have pushed all my life chips into the centre. I'm all in.

I BELIEVE THERE ARE TWO QUESTIONS THAT ARE MORE IMPORTANT THAN ANY OTHER IN HELPING US FIND OUR STORY. THOSE QUESTIONS ARE: 'WHO IS GOD?' AND 'WHO AM I?'

Chapter eight

CHARACTERS

I am a child of God, one in whom Christ dwells, and I am living in the unshakable kingdom of God.

James Bryan Smith

Moving house makes you realize just how much stuff you have. It's incredible, particularly now having children, how stuff seems to breed more stuff. We live in a consumeristic society, and I am often intrigued by the minimalist movement that has emerged over recent years. The basic premise is that we have too many possessions and we assign too much meaning to the things we own, sometimes forsaking real relationships. Minimalism is about getting rid of the excess and in the process reprioritizing what is really important in life. People who adopt this philosophy often make some quite radical changes to their lives.

One suggestion is that you box up everything in your home, as if you were about to move house. You then take items out of the boxes one at a time as and when you need them. After three months, whatever is left in the boxes you can dispose of at the charity shop because the odds are that these things are superfluous to everyday living. Other minimalist ideas include having only 100 things; whenever you buy anything new, you must dispose of something. Another philosophy is that if an item can be replaced for under £15 in under 15 minutes, then we should get rid of it. Minimalism recognizes that we tend to hoard things 'just in case', yet we may very rarely need them. Minimalism admits that there's nothing inherently wrong with owning material possessions, but that there is freedom in simplicity, in owning just a few.

As we have been exploring the idea of story, it might be that your head is swimming with different questions and ideas and thoughts. What is my underlying explanation for why we are here? Why do I hold this viewpoint? What is my story all about? To cut through all the noise, I believe there are two questions that are more important than any other in helping us find our story. Those questions are: 'Who is God?' and 'Who am I?' Let's tackle these one at a time.

WHO IS GOD?

In chapter six I outlined the God story that we find in the Bible, which gave us a window into the character of God. Many of us, though, carry one of two stereotypes of how we see God. Even having read that chapter we can find these images hard to shift.

Some of us picture a distant God sitting up on a cloud, fuming with anger. We imagine him armed with bolts of lightning, looking down upon us with disappointment and disdain, watching for the next time we make a mistake. The other stereotype is to think of God as a bit like Santa. He's safe and fuzzy and is someone we just come to with our requests, which he may or may not answer. We see God as always there but he isn't really noticed or remembered except at special times of the year.

Both these pictures miss what the God of the Bible is like. And 2,000 years ago the people of Israel also had some misconceptions about the character of God. So, with both the religious leaders and ordinary people within earshot, Jesus tells one of the most famous stories ever told (Luke 15.11–32).

It begins with a familiar scenario – a father who has two sons. But the trajectory of the story takes an almighty turn as the younger son asks for his inheritance early. He wants to live his own story now, without having to wait around for the cash that will one day arrive with his father's death. It's an audacious request, as the young son is basically saying, 'Dad, I wish you were dead.'

The listening crowd would have been captivated, waiting for the father to bring his son back to reality with an enthusiastic rebuttal. But then the father does the unthinkable. He gives the younger son his inheritance. The crowd would have gasped. What kind of a father does this?

The younger son goes on his way, living his own story, away from the shadow of home. He is living the happiness narrative, living for the moment. Sex, drugs and rock and roll. Until one day the money runs out. He finds himself bankrupt just as a recession hits. He is forced to do the lowliest of jobs, feeding pigs while his pangs of hunger are so bad he longs to fill himself with their food. Coming to his senses and with his grovelling apology rehearsed, he heads home hoping to become a servant for his father. He has realized that his autonomous story was not all it was cracked up to be.

The crowd would have lapped this up. This humiliated young man was on his way home to get some hard medicine. But then, as he arrives on the horizon, his father is watching and waiting for him. The son tries to get his words of apology out but his father is hearing none of it. He is just thrilled to have his son back as he welcomes him with a warm embrace.

The father continues to show the son extravagant love, giving him sandals and a ring and a robe, which powerfully symbolize his reinstatement into the family. He is being welcomed home and a party is to be held to celebrate.

It's as the party is getting into full swing that the older son reappears. When he finds out about the fuss being made over his brother, who has squandered his portion of the inheritance, he kicks off. The father leaves the festivities to attend to the older son. And with the sound of the party there in the background the older son grills his father. The father is full of joy and explains that what has been lost has now been found. This is something worth celebrating. But the older son just can't see it and refuses to participate.

It's this kind of story that got Jesus into trouble. It would have really annoyed the religious leaders. They would have quickly identified that the father was God and that they, who kept the religious laws and regulations, were represented by the older son.

In their minds, God would not have welcomed the wayward son back because that would have been an embarrassment. But the ordinary people would have marvelled at this story. If the father welcomed the younger son back so willingly, then perhaps they too could be welcomed back into God's presence.

This story has been celebrated throughout the centuries by artists and songwriters and poets. It depicts so powerfully the character of God. He is a good Father. He is abounding in love. He gives us freedom to make our decisions. He is patient and kind and generous and warm. He wants to welcome us home when we have been wayward.

It's in this short story that Jesus gives us a vivid picture of the big story. This is the God story told through the pages of the whole Bible squeezed into the tangibility of an intimate family setting. And in it we see that God is not sitting on a cloud, distant and angry, nor is he just a benign Santa.

God is not distant; it is we who are distant. We are still trying to create our own story away from God. We fill our lives with things that have little meaning. Some of us claim the God story, but then like the older brother live our lives with an air of superiority and never really allow the Father's love to consume us.

God is not fuelled by anger. Ultimately, he is fuelled by love. Psalm 103.8 says that God is 'slow to anger, abounding in love', but for many years I struggled with the idea of God being angry at all. Over time I came to the conclusion that if God was never angry then I could not worship him. I needed him to be angry about the way things are – with injustice and greed and abuse and imperfection. And I now realize that this means that I need God to be angry with my attitudes and actions too, both when I am like the younger brother selfishly chasing my own agenda and when I am like the older brother, living in smug pride.

And God is not just a safe gift-giver. He can't be boxed up and contained. C. S. Lewis, in his classic *The Lion, the Witch and the Wardrobe*, writes this brilliant line. In talking about Aslan, who represents God, the children ask Mr Beaver whether Aslan is safe. And Mr Beaver answers, 'Safe? Who said anything about safe? 'Course he isn't safe. But he's good. He's the King, I tell you.'

The father in this story is the unchanging God who created everything and longs for intimacy and harmony and partnership. And as we immerse ourselves in the pages of the God story, we begin to discover the character of God.

WHO AM I?

Now to the second question. One of the greatest consequences of that first decision made in the first garden is that we no longer fully recognize who we are. We are defined by circumstance rather than by the very essence of our being.

We may feel we have had a good life so far. We may be defined by our beauty or our ability or our success. But there will come a time when looks fade, our abilities fail and we endure failures. How then do we define ourselves? Or we may feel that our life so far has been quite tough. Perhaps we are defined by our imperfection or our inability or our problems. We can spend our lives trying to change our circumstances in order to change how we perceive our identity.

For some of us, finding a story for our lives can be all about trying to manufacture the right circumstances so that we can truly be at one with who we are. If we have just the right friends and family and experiences and things, then we'll be happy. If we have the right bank balance and the right sense of security, then we will finally feel safe. If we have made an impact on the world, made our mark in history in just the right way, then we will feel that we are significant. But the ultimate truth is that our identity is not formulated by the external but by the internal. Our circumstances ultimately don't change our identity.

I have friends who have changed career and moved continents with the idea that if their circumstances change then life will be better. But they discover that their perceived identity does not change after all, because they have not done the hard work in exploring who they are but instead simply changed their surroundings.

I have recently taken up boxing. We play football, we play badminton and we play table tennis, but boxing is one of the few sports you don't *play*. You don't play boxing. In a gym built in an underground tunnel, in a room soaked with the stale smell of sweat, the training is intense. Boxing is the type of sport that creates powerful stories. There is a clearly defined character, a need and an obvious conflict. Our coach, Bill, now in his sixties, is abnormally hard for his years and as fit as any personal trainer. Each session he inspires us budding boxers with stories, to help us endure the painful workouts and hours of sparring.

He once told us about a group of new boxers that he was preparing for their first fight. At one particularly intense training session – a cocktail of burpees, press-ups and squats – some of the group felt they could no longer take the pace. A barrage of excuses rolled in, along the lines of, 'I haven't had enough sleep', and 'Work has been so hectic recently'. One by one, they began to quit and sat out to recover.

But there was one woman who kept powering through, the agony obvious on her sweat-covered face. She was exhausted but she persevered. At the end of the session Bill went around the room asking each individual what their excuse was for giving up and sitting out. They all had their answers. Except her. 'I have no excuse,' she said. Later it turned out that she had just gone through cancer treatment, yet she had come to training. She had the best excuse of them all, except she chose not to share it. She wanted to power through. 'I have no excuse.'

Our circumstances are often our excuses. We allow our situation to define us and excuse our attitude, our character, our very being. But the God story is like a right hook that confronts our understanding of who we are. Rather than trying to switch our circumstances, first and foremost the God story reveals that we have an identity in God. And when we allow this reality to sink in, allowing God to do some heart surgery on us, everything can change.

The God story shows us what is wrong with how we view ourselves. The Gospels, as they tell the life of Jesus, demonstrate what this confrontation is like. For example, there was a woman who had been bleeding for 12 years (Mark 5.24–34). She was ostracized by her community and unable to participate in corporate worship. She had spent all her money on doctors searching for a cure, but to no avail. One day, hearing that Jesus is in town, she squeezes her way through the crowd. She has heard about the miracles and is desperate to be healed. She reaches out to touch the hem of his garment and is miraculously made well.

And then there is a really awkward moment. She probably thinks she can disappear back into the crowd without being noticed, but Jesus stops, turns round and asks who touched his garment. When I read this story I often think, why did Jesus need to make such a public spectacle of this lady? She could have kept quiet, but instead, full of fear, she steps forward and kneels at the feet of Jesus. She tells him her life story and he responds with these words: 'Daughter, your faith has healed you. Go in peace . . .'

Jesus calls her 'daughter'. This woman who has been barred from society has not only been healed but been welcomed back into the community. She has been shown her value and her worth. No longer defined by her circumstance, her identity is reframed by the words of Jesus.

Another story found in the Gospels doesn't end quite so beautifully. It's of a rich young ruler (Matthew 19.16–22). Those three words defined his identity in Jewish culture. The fact that he was rich was often assumed to be a sign that God had blessed him. He was young, his years full of potential. And he was a man with power.

He comes to Jesus asking about eternal life. He comes to the right person with the right question. Together they talk about keeping the religious laws, which the young man believes he is doing pretty well. Then Jesus, full of love for this man, tells him, 'One thing you lack: go, sell your possessions and give to the poor, and you will have treasure in heaven. Then come, follow me.' On hearing these words, the rich young ruler becomes sad. You can almost imagine the colour draining from his face. The passage says that he went away grieving. He had such a great property portfolio that he was unwilling to make such a radical decision. He remained defined by his circumstances.

I believe that the God story confronts how we view ourselves, and it's in this confrontation that we find freedom. We discover that we are not defined by circumstance, but by a Creator who was so desperate for us to know our true identity that he sent Jesus to change completely the trajectory of our stories.

A NEW IDENTITY

Every day we see hundreds of symbols. Symbols are extremely useful. When we're driving, symbols on signs denote danger and hazards. When we're hungry there are symbols that help us work out what to eat. Whether we are washing our clothes, reading a map or using our smartphone, symbols are all around us.

The God story is full of symbols too, the most common one being the cross. Baptism is one of the most powerful symbols. In ancient Jewish tradition ritual purification was carried out by priests and symbolized people becoming 'clean' in relation to the Jewish law, the water washing away their impurities, their shortcomings, their shame. And in the Gospels we find a man called John who picks up on this tradition. He quickly becomes known as John the Baptist, as he immerses people in the Jordan river, calling them back to the ways of God.

One of the most dramatic images in the Bible is Jesus being baptized by John. As Jesus was perfect, you may wonder why he even needed to get baptized. But it was in this moment that he was purposefully identifying himself with the people as he started out on his three years of ministry. When John pulls Jesus back up through the surface of the water, we glimpse again the three-in-one God. Jesus stands dripping in the river, a dove appears in the sky representing the Holy Spirit, and we hear the voice of the Father declare, 'This is my Son, whom I love.' The true identity of Jesus is made crystal clear to all who are present. In these words God the Father declares not only who Jesus is but also the love that connects them. The language of Father and Son helps us begin to understand the beauty and complexity of the Trinity.

And when Jesus' disciples ask him how to pray, he responds with what we commonly call the Lord's Prayer. It begins with the words 'Our Father'. These familiar words, when you dwell on them, reveal a radical approach to the Creator God. The God story contains a whole host of ways of trying to convey the relationship between God and humanity, but the notion of father is both consistent and provocative.

Being baptized is about identifying ourselves with Jesus, with God as our Father. Throughout the New Testament this symbol keeps cropping up, and in some of Jesus' final words to his followers he challenges them to 'go and make disciples, baptizing them in the name of the Father, the Son and the Holy Spirit'. Jesus obviously saw this symbolic act as important. The early Church continued with this tradition and so do we to this day. There is something beautiful about baptism – not just a cultural tradition but a symbolic act that represents the washing away of sin. It represents transformation, new life, a new story.

Paul explores the symbol of baptism in his letter to the Christian community in Rome. He uses it to explain what this new life means. He writes, 'Don't you know that all of us who were baptized into Christ Jesus were baptized into his death? We were therefore buried with him through baptism into death in order that, just as Christ was raised from the dead through the glory of the Father, we too may live a new life' (Romans 6.3–4). In essence, Paul is saying that Jesus' story becomes our story. Jesus' death and resurrection are recreated as an individual goes under the water, symbolizing death, and then brought back through the surface of the water symbolizing a new life.

Accepting the God story is about identifying on such a deep level with Jesus that not only do we recognize that we have been forgiven, but as we are immersed we acknowledge the death of ourselves at the centre of the story. We die to our failings. We die to our selfishness. We die to our greed and our pride and our hate. And we don't only say goodbye to the old life, we accept the new life that Jesus offers us. We realize our true identity and our place in his unfolding story. As we come bursting from under the water and take that first deep breath, we are making a statement that we want to embrace this new life.

As Jesus rose from the grave triumphant and victorious, we share in that same glory. As we emerge from the water, we are making a profound statement of our identity in Jesus. Jesus rose from the dead, and we share in this new eternal life. Baptism is a symbol that says we are no longer the centre of the story – but God is. We are submitting to him to work in us, shaping us and moulding us.

REMEMBERING WHO WE ARE

I don't suppose Leonard Cohen ever imagined the impact his song would have. He had been sitting, in his underwear, on the floor of his room in the Royalton Hotel in New York, for hours. A perfectionist and frustrated to the point of banging his head on the floor, he crafted 80 draft verses for the song 'Hallelujah'.

The song has been used in countless film soundtracks and sung in countless versions by the likes of KD Lang, Bono, Bob Dylan and Jeff Buckley. Each artist seems to offer an individual style and interpretation. For some it is a song of joy and celebration; others sing it with solemnity and fragility. For some it is about the struggle for spiritual wisdom, for others it is about sexuality and relationships. I find it fascinating how the song resonates with so many people. It's partly the powerful musical mix of gospel and rock and roll, but it's also something about the lyrics. The word 'hallelujah' simply means 'God be praised'. For Cohen, who had a Jewish background and meddled with a range of different faiths, the song 'explains that many kinds of hallelujahs do exist'.

This song feels pertinent to me because in all our lives there are crossroads and choices to be made. We need to decide who we will worship, who we will sing our hallelujah to. For Cohen there was a carnal hallelujah and a religious hallelujah. Each day we choose who we want to praise, whether we celebrate earthly things or sing praises to the God of the God story.

The hard thing is, it can be challenging to remember who God is. We easily get distracted when life is good and things are going well. During seasons of heavenly bliss we quickly begin to believe that we are masters of our own destiny. It can also be challenging to remember who God is when we are experiencing harrowing times. When life is painful we can end up wrestling with how a God of love, a God who is all-powerful, can let terrible things happen. And when we lose track of who God is, we can quickly lose track of who we are. We slip back into old habits and again begin to define ourselves according to much smaller stories.

The Jewish people had times in their history when they forgot who God was and who they were. When they were a great nation, when everything was going well, it was easy to put their trust in chariots and armies rather than in God, choosing to believe that they were a self-made empire. And when they were a displaced people living under heathen conqueror, when everything was going to pot, it was easy to forget God's promises and faithfulness, and live under the narrative of being a forgotten people.

It was during these times of competing narratives that they were distracted from who God was. When God gave the Jewish people a command to celebrate the Passover each year, it was to remember just who he is and who they are. This annual feast is rich in sensory symbols and helps Jews remember their escape from Egypt some 3,500 years ago. Their story is remembered as they taste bitter herbs, reminding them of their bondage in Egypt. Salty water is drunk to remind them of the tears they shed and their escape through the Red Sea. And as they celebrate the feast these words are recited: 'This year we eat in the year of bondage, next year in the Land of Promise.'

Two thousand years ago, Jesus was celebrating Passover with his disciples in an upper room. He had been looking forward to this meal but he also knew what lay ahead. As Jesus takes the unleavened bread, which symbolized the hurry with which the Israelites had left Egypt, he suddenly goes off script. He begins to redefine these ancient symbols. Breaking the bread, he says, 'This is my body given for you.' The disciples would have been baffled by this. And as he takes the wine, which symbolized the goats' blood the Israelites put on their doorposts in Egypt, he says, 'This is my blood shed for you. This is my covenant.' Now covenants were always sealed in animal blood, but Jesus was talking about his own blood. You can imagine the confusion. But in the days that followed, Jesus demonstrated the sacrifice he was talking about. His words became action.

And this is why we celebrate Communion today. It stems back to this ancient meal that Jesus shared with his closest friends. This meal is wrapped up in a story, a story about bread and wine but actually about Jesus' body and blood. This ancient ceremony reminds us of who God is and who we are. I have shared this simple meal, taking bread from shiny serving dishes and drinking from pristine goblets, in beautiful cathedrals. And I have shared it with persecuted Christians who use the simplicity of grapes, their skin representing the body of Jesus and their juice the blood.

This meal is leveller. It reminds us that God has a story, that he so longs for intimacy and harmony and partnership that he allowed Jesus to go to the cross. It reminds us that God is just and loving and present, and it reminds us that we are loved. As I share this simple meal with high-flying millionaires and homeless drug addicts, we are all equal in his sight.

BECOMING WHO WE ARE

One of the greatest artists who ever lived, Michelangelo was a painter, an architect, a poet and an engineer. He was also a sculptor. I find it hard to imagine how he was able to take a block of marble, looking for the lines and feeling the texture, and know how to begin chiselling away. His *Statue of an Angel* is half a metre high and sits proudly in the Basilica of San Domenico in Bologna. It's a fine piece of artistry with intricate detail, created out of one solid piece of marble. People have marvelled at how he was able to create such art. In a letter to a fellow artist, he explains, 'I saw the angel in the marble and carved until I set it free.'

What amazing vision, to be able to see something so beautiful hidden away in a block of rock. What he saw enabled him to work away painstakingly and tirelessly to remove the unnecessary sections of marble, both big sections and fine lines, to create his masterpiece.

Ultimately, the God story declares that there is a God who created each of us. At times we may appear to be more like a block of clay than a block of marble, but God is at work in helping us discover our true identity. It's as he removes the unnecessary bits, as he brings revolution to our hearts, chipping away at the greed and the selfishness and the pride, that we begin to discover just who we are called to be.

IT'S IN THE GOD
STORY THAT WE
DISCOVER THAT OUR
PREVIOUS STORIES
ARE TOO SMALL.

Chapter nine

WHAT GOD WANTS

The greatest issue facing the world today, with all its heartbreaking needs, is whether those who, by profession or culture, are identified as 'Christians' will become disciples – students, apprentices, practitioners – of Jesus Christ, steadily learning from him how to live the life of the Kingdom of the Heavens into every corner of human existence.

Dallas Willard

NASA spends extensive amounts of money and time preparing astronauts for the reality of space, so that when they get there they know just what to expect. Probably the most infamous preparatory practice is the 'Vomit Comet', which is a plane journey in a reduced-gravity aircraft. It prepares astronauts for zero gravity, and includes 25 seconds of weightlessness as the plane drops from the sky. In this moment, astronauts experience something of space.

But one thing that NASA is unable to prepare astronauts for is the smell of space. Space apparently has a strong odour and astronauts struggle to find the vocabulary to describe it. Space shuttle pilot

Tony Antonelli says, 'Space definitely has a smell that's different than anything else,' while Thomas Jones explains that it 'carries a distinct odour of ozone, a faint acrid smell'. So even though NASA has long been interested in reproducing the smell of space, recruiting scent specialists to work on the project, as yet they have been unable to do so.

As we live between the now and not yet of the God story, the prayer that Jesus taught us to pray contains these words: 'Your kingdom come, your will be done.' NASA scientists try to give astronauts an experience of space while living on earth. Christians are charged with praying that God's heavenly reign would come to earth.

The term Christian actually means 'little Christ'; Christ comes from the Greek word *christos*, meaning 'anointed one'. As Jesus Christ was anointed by the Holy Spirit for his mission on earth, so we are anointed to be the hands and feet of Jesus, bringing about change and transformation here on earth. NASA gives astronauts a taster of space on earth. We are charged with giving people an opportunity to discover the beauty of heaven.

GOD'S STORY IS BIGGER

Hermit crabs are fascinating creatures. Their golden-orange features make them vulnerable to both predators and the strong sunlight that can cook them alive. And so they inhabit shells. They have developed an abdomen that can clasp strongly onto the columella shell and they have the ability to tuck their legs safely inside when there is trouble lurking.

But then as they grow they quickly outgrow their shells and need to find bigger ones. Biologists have recorded the most intriguing video of what happens when a new seashell arrives on the beach. The crabs gather near to the washed ashore shell and size each other up. They form a line, in size order, from the biggest to the smallest, and then begin a chain of home exchange. When the biggest crab moves into the new shell, all the others hurriedly vacate their own shell and move into their neighbour's now available one. They each find a new home.

It's in the God story that we discover that our previous stories are too small. Like hermit crabs finding a bigger home, we need to find a bigger story to live in. The smaller stories put ourselves at the centre with an insatiable desire for what is unattainable. But with the God story we begin to see the world from a completely different perspective. We begin to see what God wants. And as we do so the stories of happiness, safety and significance are revealed to be little more than smoke and mirrors. As we examine the God meta-narrative, we actually discover that God deals with these much smaller stories.

COMPLETED STORIES

The happiness story can look so seductive. But as I have argued, happiness is a mirage that is undefinable. It's a destination that never fully exists. There will always be suffering and pain and brokenness as we live out our lives on earth. Happiness doesn't work as the *raison d'être* for our life story.

And here is an interesting thing. The Bible talks loads about joy and happiness, but in the Church we sometimes try to divide these two words, thinking of happiness as bad and joy as good. In the pages of the Bible, though, these words are often used inter-changeably. I believe that in the God story we are offered both happiness and joy.

Jesus is with his twelve followers in an upper room. The countdown is on to the crucifixion and Jesus is teaching them about what it means to remain linked to him. He talks about love and obedience. And he talks about joy – even as he is about to go to the cross. He says, 'I have told you this so that my joy may be in you and that your joy may be complete' (John 15.11). Jesus is basically claiming that his followers will know joy if they stick with him. Here's the key – their focus is not joy and happiness. Their focus is Jesus and love and obedience; joy and happiness are a spin-off.

The book of Acts in the New Testament tells the stories of the early Christians after Jesus has commissioned them and ascended into heaven. This group of believers end up in all kinds of holy mischief. They are imprisoned, beaten and murdered. On the surface their lives don't look very happy. And yet, when they are suffering immensely, we see something unusual. We see them 'rejoicing'. A good example of this is the story of Paul and Silas, two missionaries who are sharing about Jesus in Greece. Their actions negatively affect the local economy and they are arrested, stripped, beaten and thrown into prison. But then, even in prison, naked and vulnerable with their bodies covered with deep bruising and congealed blood, they begin singing and praying (Acts 16.25).

What's interesting about this story is that it shows us that joy and happiness, which come from finding our life in God's story, are not determined by external circumstances. Joy and happiness from God are cultivated internally, as we make peace with who we are and as we find our identity in God and not in other people, in holidays, nights out or material possessions.

Solomon was a great king of Israel who lived many hundreds of years before Jesus. He was one of the most powerful and richest men in history, and he was known for his wisdom. He explored all the world had to offer in the pursuit of happiness. And he says that he found it lacking. '"Laughter," I said, "is foolish. And what does pleasure accomplish?"' (Ecclesiastes 2.2). He discovered that the joy and happiness that the world had to offer was a mirage, but the joy found in God was rich and abundant. And the Bible promises, as we allow the Holy Spirit, part of this three-in-one God, to come into our lives, that we will receive joy (Galatians 5.22). This is not temporary but eternal.

The happiness narrative that many people choose to live for is all about chasing the things that promise to make us feel good. The God story is about chasing after God, and as we do so we discover his joy and happiness in our lives. The Christian monastic communities have long understood this. They have developed practices and rhythms and rituals that help them avoid getting caught up in the happiness narrative, instead allowing them to flourish as part of God's story. Their simple lives lay down a profound challenge to many of us in the Western world.

Their rhythms of prayer allow them to appreciate and be thankful for what they have. They have committed to timetables that allow them to be 'present' in the moment. And they have chosen to live lives of generosity, with an understanding that possessions can separate us, and what is essential is community. Their lives together are centred around God.

Then there's the safety story. Again, feeling secure has its appeal, but as we know, no one is ever safe. Our life story, measured in days, months and years, can be cut short at any moment. And ultimately, living a story in search of security can rob us of the adventure of life.

My friend from Ethiopia fled to the UK as a refugee, fearing for his life. He explains how when he arrived in the country he was desperate for security. Once in the UK he moved in among other Ethiopians in London. He kept himself to himself, trying to look after his own, and better his family's situation. But one day he had a realization that he was not in the UK just to take and consume and to be safe. He discovered that God was calling him to be an agent of change in his new environment. As we met over good strong Ethiopian coffee, he spoke about this revelation as being like a new way of seeing the world. And since this epiphany, he has begun to live a far riskier, life-giving story as he seeks to build local community and encourage ethnic cohesion through local festivals and performing arts programmes.

He has stepped out of his comfortable cultural circle and has risked sharing his dreams with others such as community stake-holders, and has brought together segments of the community that had never previously been connected. He is now known as a mover and shaker because he is no longer confined to the safety narrative.

At the heart of the God story, as we find our identity as children loved by God we are freed from some of the fears that steal away our best stories. When we solely want to look out for ourselves, we are validated by what others think of us and the comfort that money and resources bring. But when we discover God's love in the God story, we can become more vulnerable, become truly known. Finally, there is the significance story.

Christopher Wren, the architect behind St Paul's Cathedral, is buried on the site of the cathedral. A Latin inscription in the great building translates, 'Reader, if you seek his memorial, look around you.' Wren built 51 churches in London after the Great Fire in 1666, but St Paul's is his masterpiece.

There is a story that on the building site one morning, incognito, Wren stopped three different workers, all doing the same task, to ask them what they were doing. The three labourers each gave a different response. 'I am cutting this stone,' said the first. The second worker responded, 'I am earning three shillings six pence a day.' And the third labourer stood up straight and declared, 'I am helping Sir Christopher Wren build this great cathedral.'

Each of the three workers had a different way of seeing their role, but the third worker knew that he was doing something significant. It's in the God story that we also find significance. We, like the labourer, discover that we are part of something so much larger than the stone we are cutting or the wage we are earning.

When we realize that we have a role to play in God's arching narrative, we find that the decisions we make and the things we do are significant. Every interaction we make leaves a trace and as we go about life we leave people with a taster of eternity, with the scent of another world. Significance does not always mean prominence but it does mean that our lives matter, whether our role is as a leading character or as a behind-the-scenes runner.

Hermit crabs continually grow and need bigger shells, but the same is not true for us. As we discover the enormity of God's narrative, we no longer need to look for bigger stories. God's narrative is as vast as time itself. In this story we find joy and happiness, but not as the world might define it. And in this story we find security, not necessarily in terms of having a decent pension, but in loving God who is for us. And in this story we find significance, defined not by our own ideas but by a story that spans eternity.

This might seem to be making sense conceptually, but the challenging question is how, as we go through the different seasons of life, do we begin to tease out our calling? What does our subplot in God's great story really look like?

WHERE THE RUBBER HITS THE ROAD

Finding our own subplot doesn't necessarily mean becoming a monk or training to be a vicar. It is about discovering how we can shape the world around us as we partner with God. It's about being ambassadors, giving people an experience of the kingdom of God.

It's about spiritual change, helping others discover who God is and something about their true worth and identity. It's about social change, transforming structures and institutions so that people are empowered to live well, free from the strongholds of poverty. And it's about cultural change, creating in our different spheres of influence a better way of being.

It might be about seeing other people become fully alive, as they explore their creativity through the arts; or wanting to see children in the classroom thrive and be released into meaningful lives. It might be about creating financial resources to reinvest into social enterprises that give families a future. A good subplot needs to have a noble ambition that goes beyond selfishness and serves God's kingdom priorities.

History is littered with stories of ordinary men and women who have discovered their purpose. In the eighteenth century, Johann Sebastian Bach, widely regarded as one of the greatest composers of all time, found his story in God's story. He wrote the words 'Soli Deo gloria' on every page of every piece of music he composed, a Latin term that means 'for the Glory of God alone'. His music was his response to God. His story was a subplot in God's story.

But perhaps my favourite story is that of the Cadbury family. One hundred and seventy years ago it was impossible to buy a chocolate bar. Chocolate was already big business, but it was sold in blocks of fatty paste and bits were crumbled off and mixed with milk or water to form a drink. Richard and George Cadbury, who took on their father's struggling cocoa business in 1861, had a vision to make Cadbury's great.

The odds were stacked against them. They were dwarfed by bigger UK cocoa companies and both the Swiss and the Dutch were creating superior products having made huge technological advances. The failing Cadbury business lacked the capital needed to improve their production processes that were crammed into a small factory in the heart of Birmingham.

This was a dark period of British history. The Industrial Revolution had trapped vast swathes of the population in poverty. Slums had blossomed in the booming cities and drunkenness provided the only escape from a dire existence. Children found themselves in lives of slavery – boys and sometimes girls as young as five were used by chimney sweeps to navigate their way up chimney shafts as small as seven square inches.

The Cadbury brothers, like their father, held a vision bigger than producing great cocoa products. Their vision was reform. George Cadbury had seen that 'machinery creates wealth but destroys men'. The brothers aimed to tackle the slums of Britain and rescue children trapped in poverty. Even the cocoa drink held a vision to create a nutritious alternative to alcohol. The business modelled their values from the outset. They provided sick pay, taught their staff to read and write, arranged staff outings and introduced half days on Saturdays. They took up all manner of causes to fight for the oppressed.

With this bigger story driving them forward, the chocolate business was their vehicle for reform. They risked all their inheritance money to rescue the failing business. Despite various setbacks and a catalogue of bereavements, the Cadburys survived the nineteenth century. An array of new products, ranging from Cocoa Essence to The Fancy Box, began to challenge other

British cocoa companies. The wealth they created was invested in modelling an alternative to the slums that plagued Britain.

In 1879 the Cadburys launched 'a factory in a garden'. The concept was a factory away from the cramped slums, with open space and fresh air to fill the lungs. Bournville was birthed, just south of Birmingham, alongside the new railway tracks. The factory was soon surrounded by a new village complete with sports facilities. By 1900 there were 370 cottages providing affordable homes for both workers and the general public. Each home had enough land to grow food and could therefore offer inhabitants an opportunity for a healthy lifestyle. As George Cadbury declared, 'We must destroy the slums of England or England will be destroyed by the slums.' Their model was influential and replicated around the UK.

It wasn't until 1905 that Cadbury's Dairy Milk was finally launched. The new product seriously challenged the Swiss and Dutch monopoly; today it is regularly enjoyed in 33 countries around the globe. By that time Richard had died and George had handed over the business to the next generation. But the legacy continued.

What made the Cadbury story great? The Cadbury brothers knew how to work hard. They also knew the importance of innovation, always pursuing new concepts and ideas. They utilized new technologies, invested in advertising and saw the importance of global exports to places as far afield as Australia and Burma as early as 1888. But perhaps what we can really learn from the Cadbury story is the brothers' commitment to a story bigger than themselves. Their story was not about personal wealth. In fact, they led meagre lives. Their story was about change for the better. They wanted to create wealth to bless their community. They understood the responsibility and accountability that came with the gift of life.

Throughout their adventures in chocolate, they held dear the Christian ideal that life should be lived with truth, honesty and justice. At the deepest level, they applied the teaching of Jesus to all areas of their lives.

DISCOVERING YOUR PURPOSE

When we choose the God story, we become wrapped up in showing the world how God intended things to be. Paul explains this concept using the illustration of ambassadors – people sent by one sovereign to another to represent their interests (2 Corinthians 5.20). When we realize that our identity isn't ultimately in the story of our ambition or our culture or our country, but is first and foremost in the God story, we discover that we take on an ambassadorial role. Our identity in God's story means that we are citizens in God's kingdom and on earth we are his ambassadors. We have a mission and an authority that stems from the King.

In the God story, we find out not only who God is and who we are but also what God wants – namely intimacy and harmony and partnership. And it's as we realize what God wants that we begin to discover our purpose here on earth. We are not to sit around waiting until the day we get transported to heaven; we are to experience and to give other people an experience of heaven on earth.

God wants intimacy. Part of our purpose here on earth is about reminding ourselves of the God story so that we live in God's reality rather than in the shallowness of the stories offered by the world. This is about diving into the Bible and allowing God to speak into our very being. It's about creating a rhythm of prayer that helps us become aware of who God is and who we are. And if God wants intimacy, then another part of our role is about inviting others into this relationship with him. It's about helping to remove the stumbling blocks and sharing something of what we have discovered.

God wants harmony. As we discover our identity in him, we develop the ability to see how we have failed others around us. Jesus speaks about humility, about compassion and love. This is about beginning to fix the broken relationships that we each have. And at the heart of a harmonious relationship is the need for forgiveness. When Jesus was quizzed by one of his followers about how many times he needed to forgive someone who had hurt him, Jesus responded with a powerful story of a king who wanted to sort out his accounts (Matthew 18.21–35).

One of the king's servants had a huge debt to pay – running into the millions. The servant is unable to pay it back and so the king orders that he and his family should be sold off as slaves. The servant responds by throwing himself at the king's feet, begging for mercy. The king mercifully relents and cancels the debt. The servant leaves the king's presence and immediately comes across another servant who only owes him about four months' worth of wages. This servant can't pay him, and begs for mercy. But rather than showing him the same grace the king has shown him, he throws the servant in prison. The king finds out what has happened and is outraged. He summons the servant: 'You wicked servant! I forgave your entire debt when you begged me for mercy. Shouldn't you be compelled to be merciful to your fellow servant who asked for mercy?'

As God has forgiven us and brought harmony between us, we are called to do the same. Jesus famously said, 'Blessed are the peace-makers, for they will be called the children of God' (Matthew 5.9). It's in bringing harmony that people recognize our Father in heaven.

And finally, God wants partnership. He wants to work in us, with us and through us. From the very beginning of the Genesis story we were designed for more than a relationship with God. We were designed for relationship with one another and for a role within creation.

God's kingdom, his reign here on earth, is about the transform-ation of all things, and God chooses to use us to bring about his transformation. The role of the Holy Spirit, the third person of God, is not just to give us a warm fuzzy feeling when we sing songs of worship but to empower us to see change here on earth.

The God story is about the Holy Spirit leading us and prompting us into action. Our actions do not earn God's favour, but they are a response to all he is and all he has done.

ALTHOUGH WE ARE ALL MADE IN THE IMAGE OF GOD, EACH OF US IS UNIQUE AND WE ALL HAVE A PART TO PLAY.

Chapter ten

YOUR UNIQUE SUBPLOT

So do you want to make culture? Find a community, a small group who can lovingly fuel your dreams and puncture your illusions. Find friends and form a family who are willing to see grace at work in one another's lives, who can discern together which gifts and which crosses each has been called to bear. Find people who have a holy respect for power and a holy willingness to spend their power alongside the powerless. Find some partners in the wild and wonderful world beyond church doors. And then, together, make something of the world.

Andy Crouch

I love hearing the stories from the past of people who were rooted in the God story and were used to transform and change the world around them. But, you might be thinking, I am neither a great composer like Bach nor a chocolatier like the Cadburys. Choosing the God story is not about trying to be like someone else but about discovering your purpose that flows out of your true identity. You are not ultimately defined by what you do, but what you do is an expression of your true identity.

The saddest thing for me is seeing people who profess to believe in the God story and yet fail to find their unique subplot in God's unfolding narrative. They remain trapped in the comparisons that play in their head and feel unable to move forward in finding a direction or calling for their lives. As we saw in chapter one, in the making of a good story there needs to be someone who wants something. But some of the followers of Jesus I meet don't seem to want much, or indeed anything at all. They resign themselves to living rather boring stories, seemingly unaware there is an alternative, or not caring whether there is or not. When I ask why they are not living an exciting story in partnership with God there are two common responses.

The first excuse is that God has never spoken to them. The Bible is full of incredible encounters as God meets key individuals. God meets Moses at a burning bush in the desert. Burning bushes would have been quite common but this one was burning and not burning up and so it caught Moses' attention. In his profound conversation with God, Moses' desire to see his people freed from captivity is unearthed (Exodus 3—4). Another incredible encounter is when Mary is visited by the angel Gabriel. This scene as re-enacted in countless primary schools each Christmas often fails to capture the intensity of the experience – Mary is petrified as this towering supernatural being tells her that she is pregnant while still a virgin (Luke 1.26–38). And then Paul, who has been busy killing Christians, meets God in a vision of Jesus on a desert road. His entourage fall to the floor and he is temporarily blinded as he hears Jesus say, 'Why do you persecute me?' (Acts 9).

And here's the thing: perhaps people are waiting for such an encounter. But what makes these encounters incredible is that they are rare. God rarely chooses to speak through burning bushes and visiting angels and blinding light. Too many of us wander through life waiting for a pivotal moment when everything will change rather than seeing that God is prompting us in the everyday of ordinary life. If God needs you to do something I strongly believe that he will make it clear to you, if you're really listening. And if later today an angel does come through your door just as you're doing the washing up, then be attentive to what God is saying. But if there is no such angelic visitation, then God has given you the ability and freedom to discern what to do with your life.

I have never encountered God in a burning bush and at times it is frustrating trying to discern what God is saying. If God commands clearly, then we simply have the choice as to whether to obey or not. But in the absence of any specific command, whether delivered by an angel or not, then God has given us his story and his Holy Spirit to prompt us, together with the wisdom of friends, and the freedom to work it out for ourselves. It's time to stop waiting for a burning bush.

The second immobilizing excuse is being aware of the costliness of our subplot. Living out the God story is not all safe and easy. It's costly. In fact Jesus says that we need to pick up our cross to follow him. He is challenging us; just as he went to the cross, following him will not always be easy.

The cost can seem too great at times, and even while we profess the God story we default to living our three smaller stories. We sense God calling us to live a life of generosity but that happiness narrative kicks in, and instead we choose to take an extra all-inclusive holiday. We sense God calling us to stand up against some injustice, but we fear the consequences. We realize that standing up for something means standing against something, and that could be costly and so we play it safe. We sense God calling us to support someone else's endeavour but then we begin to see how little credit we will get and the significance story kicks in. We instead choose a direction that will get us more limelight.

Often it's not one big decision to turn down our subplot in God's story but a thousand little decisions we make. They can seem inconsequential but in fact they rob us of playing a role in the greatest story ever told.

First and foremost, God wants us to live in our true identity. Quite naturally, as we live from the viewpoint of how God sees us, the things we do and say will have an impact. You may be thinking right now that you have no idea what you want to do with your life. There are endless possibilities and it's hard enough working out whether to have a cappuccino or a latte. Don't worry, I've been there. Finding our subplot is often about starting small, and there are three questions that can help us navigate how we live a good story. First, what are the roles, relationships and responsibilities God has given you?

ROLES, RELATIONSHIPS AND RESPONSIBILITIES

I am a husband, a father, a son, an uncle and a neighbour. I am also a charity director and a communicator. You may be a wife or a grandparent or a stepdad or a flatmate. And you may be a teacher or a cleaner or a soldier or an administrator. The roles you have begin to give you an insight into the purposes you have right now.

If you're married, then part of your purpose is to love, support and release your partner into their story. If you are a parent, part of your role is to be lovingly present and to introduce your children to God's great story, helping them navigate the highs and lows of life. As a neighbour, you are tasked with showing love to your neighbour, going beyond the occasional hello to knowing people's names and their stories.

Our roles are in part the relationships we have and in part the things we do. Whether we are in paid employment or volunteering or studying, each of these roles has a purpose. Bach was a composer and the Cadburys were businessmen; they each used their roles to reveal something of the kingdom of God with their creativity and compassion. As we list the roles we have, the question we need to ask ourselves is what we want for each of them.

You might be thinking that you don't have much power to create purpose in the roles you have. You might feel limited in this respect, perhaps as an employee with fixed hours and assignments. But the attitude and the pride you take in the roles you have helps give them purpose. I remember during my university days working nights stacking shelves, from 11 p.m. until 8 a.m. It was a most demoralizing job. Trying to arrange packets of ladies' tights in different shades of grey and blue on a dimple wall with limited light at three in the morning was tough. But one of my colleagues, who had been doing this role for many years, was inviting and encouraging and talkative. Even in the mundanity of organizing a display of women's tights, she had a purpose.

I first came across this process of listing my roles through the writings of Donald Miller. It gave me a real insight into my purpose as a father. I already knew I was responsible for loving my children, providing for them and trying to learn the lyrics to Disney films. But in defining this role and what I wanted for my family I found clarity around what this looked like in the day to day. Understanding my roles began to make an impact on the everyday decisions I was making constantly.

On top of the roles you play at home and in the workplace, when you accept the God story you find yourself part of an amazing God community. This community that we call Church is a mixed group of young and old, rich and poor, black and white. And in this community you also have a part to play. It may be that you haven't got a key role from the front of church on a Sunday morning, but you can serve and participate in a community unlike any other.

WHAT ARE YOU PASSIONATE ABOUT?

The second key question falls into two parts. There are some things we are passionate about doing – following a football team or knitting jumpers or computer programming. Part of your purpose is wrapped up in what you love to do. But there is another element to being passionate about things. When we discover peace with God we become restless with how things are in the world. We need to take up a cause that goes beyond ourselves and is about effecting change around us.

From all around the world we are bombarded with stories of suffering: child abuse, the destruction of rainforests, extreme poverty or institutionalized racism. And it's easy to develop a hard heart. Rather than finding ourselves weeping as we read the latest news, we can become less and less affected by the brokenness in the world.

Maybe we need to take the defences down and allow God to break our hearts for the things that break his heart. Because things are not as they are supposed to be. We can pray for the brokenness of the world but we also need, in part, to become the answer to those prayers – comforting those who mourn, sipping tea with the lonely and campaigning about the injustices that enslave millions.

WHAT IS UNIQUE ABOUT YOU?

As for the third and final question, although we are all made in the image of God, each of us is unique. It's not just our finger-prints but our experiences, our abilities, our revelations and our relationships mean that we are all one of a kind. There will never be another exact replica of you and so your story is unique. And as businesses that want to perform well need to discern their unique selling point, so do we.

The trouble we often have is that we want to live other people's stories. We wish we had the roles someone else has or the passion someone else has or the unique gifting that someone else has. A friend of mine for a long time wanted to have children. He and his wife tried everything in order to get pregnant, including going through costly IVF, but they never conceived. It was so easy for him to wish that he could take on someone else's role, that he could be a father. But what's interesting is that his painful experiences have allowed him to speak into countless other situations, about infertility, disappointment and frustration. His unique struggle has given him an opportunity to communicate God's story to those who are working through similar issues.

Finding our purpose is about working through our roles. It's about allowing passion to be reignited. And it's about discovering what makes us unique. Rather than worry about what we will do, or should not do, we need to start small. And if we begin to go off in the wrong direction, with the wrong idea, we can trust that God will lovingly draw us back.

There is a strange story in the Bible about a woman called Esther. It's strange because there is no mention of God in the entirety of the book. If you have seen the film *300* you may be familiar with King Xerxes and the Persian Empire. The context of the story is that the Jewish people have been dispersed from their homeland. Many of them are living under Persian rule and Esther wins an ancient beauty contest and is chosen to be Xerxes' wife. It might sound glamorous but really she would have been almost like a modern-day sex slave married to one of the most powerful men in an extremely violent time in history.

In this short story we see a purpose being worked out. There is no burning bush or angelic visitation, but there is a plot afoot to wipe out the Jewish people. Esther has a role as queen. She is passionate about protecting her people. And she is unique in that she is extremely beautiful, wise, brave and also a keen strategist. She risks her life by entering the king's presence without invitation, for which she could be executed, daring to go into the throne room to plead for her people. While there is no overt mention of God in this small book, we see God continually at work in the story.

From the ancient story of Esther to more recent stories such as that of the Cadburys, we see that we have the opportunity to be a subplot in God's story. As we discover our role as ambassadors, bringing the scent of heaven to earth, praying 'your kingdom come', we need to know what we want.

Here's the thing: you can live a good story without knowing God. But if you want to live God's best story for your life, then you need to know the author of the story. And as you discover your identity in him, you will begin to discover your purpose.

You are not a mistake. You have been designed with a part to play. Your roles show where God has positioned you. Your passions show where God is leading you. Your uniqueness shows where God has prepared you. What will your life breathe into the world?

Some of us need to want something again. Some of us need to start wanting the right things. And some of us need to stop waiting for a burning bush.

GOD, YOU HAVE MADE US FOR YOURSELF, AND OUR HEARTS ARE RESTLESS UNTIL THEY REST IN YOU.

ST AUGUSTINE

Conclusion

There's an amazing story about a village in south India where the locals wanted to catch monkeys. Rather than trying to catch them in fancy nets, they had an innovative approach. They simply cut holes in coconuts and filled them with rice. These coconuts were fixed to a stake, close to where the monkeys convened.

Within moments the monkeys smell the rice. They find the coconuts and bury their hand inside to seize the booty. The monkey's hand fits through the hole perfectly but when the fist is clenched the monkey can't get the hand back out. As villagers approach to capture the monkey, the monkey can quickly escape but first they must let go of their handful of rice. And they don't. They are so determined to keep clutching the rice, they are immobilized and captured.

Too many of us in the Western world today are holding on tightly to stories of happiness, safety and significance. These narratives, with ourselves at the centre, are like a magician's trick. We are focusing on the wrong things and we are imprisoned in a strait-jacket that tells us we are defined by our emotions, our bank balance and our success.

Each life tells a story, but ultimately our life is a fraction of eternity. For me, I have found in the God story the place that grounds my story. I am not the key character in my story but a subplot in God's great unfolding meta-narrative. And here's what's interesting. It's in finding my subplot in God's story that I have found the three small stories, and our human desires to pursue them also begin to make sense.

Living in the God story doesn't mean that life is always easy but it does promote a sense of joy in the very depth of my being. This comes from a thankfulness to God and a sense of trusting in him that affects my entire outlook. Living in God's story does not mean that I am always safe, immune from troubles and suffering. In fact, by living the God story I sometimes find myself, humanly speaking, in more danger than I would otherwise. But his love casts out fear and there is a confidence that he is with me whatever challenge I face. And living in God's story does not mean that I always feel I am important. His story reminds me to stay humble and compassionate and obedient. God's way of doing things may not be the way I would do things, yet the God story reminds me that I have value and meaning and purpose. It's the God story that actually completes these three small stories.

A choice was made at the beginning of time as we know it – a choice in a garden. Another choice was made in another garden as Jesus chose to go to the cross, setting in motion his redemptive plans. The end of the story is clear. Not a garden but a city, and an ending full of beauty and hope that beckons us onwards. But the choice for us, living in the now and the not yet, is where will we pin our faith? What will be the story that we confidently choose to live by?

I have a confession to make. I miss Blockbuster Video. I used to love going into Blockbuster on a Friday night to choose a DVD. There was something special about thumbing the DVD cases and reading the back covers, to make the all-important choice for that night's entertainment. I wonder what the back cover of the DVD of my life would read?

Finding your subplot in God's story begins with a simple prayer, like the one I've included below. You may choose to say it for the first time, or it may be a prayer to remind you afresh of your shared and unique roles in God's unfolding story. But in any case, it is not just about that one prayer. It's about a daily choice to remember the God story and remember your role within it. It's about remembering that God is working in and through us.

There will be days when things are going well, the sun is shining and all is as it should be. There will be days when things are tough, when the sky is overcast and it seems to reflect your soul. On good days and tough days, we have a choice to make. That choice is whether or not we will sing a hallelujah of thanksgiving to God, whether we will remember whose we are and keep pursuing a life story that only really makes sense as part of God's bigger story.

Don't be fooled by illusion. Let go of the rice and embrace the God of the God story.

> Father,
> I thank you, that you're the author and centre of the 'big story'.
> I am sorry for when I have made myself the centre of the story, separating myself from you.

I give your Son Jesus, the storyteller, my life story.

I believe his death and resurrection mean that I can know you personally.

I invite Jesus to rewrite my past that I may know I am forgiven.

I invite Jesus to write my present, that I might know your peace.

And I give Jesus my future, that in following him, I will find my role in the 'big story'.

May your Spirit confirm these things.

Amen.

Your story

Thinking and praying through the following questions may help you discover what the God story means for you and your story.

What stories are you living in?

How do the happiness, the safety and the significance story make an impact on the way you live?

Whose life stories inspire you?

What story would you like your life to tell?

What risks would you take if you were unafraid?

What are your reflections on the God story as you work through the Dream, the Reality and Spoiler Rooms?

Who is God? What is his character?

Who are you? What does God think?

Reflect on your roles, relationships and responsibilities . . .

What are you passionate about?

What is unique about you?

How can you better embrace your subplot in God's story?

Notes

1 Bobette Buster, 'The Arc of Storytelling', Q Conference, 2014 <www.youtube.com/watch?v=WaflgyRA5qQ>.

2 James Bryan Smith, *The Good and Beautiful God* (London: Hodder, 2011), pp. 24–5.

3 Allison Schmitt, Local 4 TV interview <www.clickondetroit.com/family/cantons-allison-schmitt-speaks-candidly-about-post-olympic-depression>.

4 Russell Brand, *Revolution* (London: Century, 2014), p. 51.